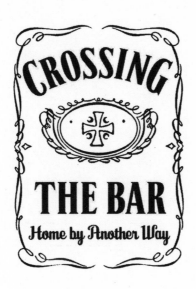

CROSSING

THE BAR

Home by Another Way

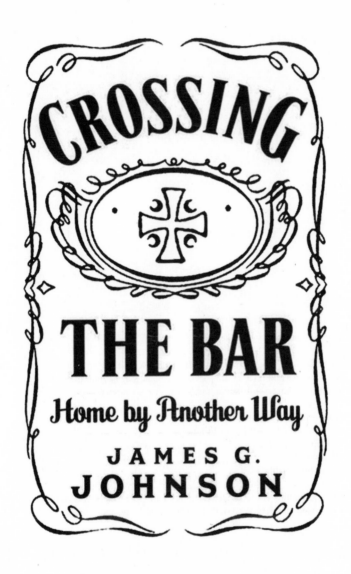

CROSSING THE BAR

Home by Another Way

JAMES G. JOHNSON

CHURCH
INNOVATIONS
PUBLISHING

Crossing the Bar: Home by another Way

Published in St Paul, Minnesota by
Church Innovations Institute, Incorporated
1563 Como Avenue #103
St Paul, Mn 55108
www.churchinnovations.org

Scripture quotations unless otherwise marked are from The New Oxford Annotated Bible—Revised Standard Version © 1977 by Oxford University Press

First edition 2010
Cover & interior design: Lookout Design, Inc. (www.lookoutdesign.com)

ISBN: 0-9829313-0-1
ISBN 13: 978-0-9829313-0-1
Printed in the United States of America

17 16 15 14 13 12 11 10   1 2 3 4 5 6 7 8

FOREWORD

I envy you the chance to read the stories in this book for the first time. I have heard these stories and known many of these people for over twenty years through your guide and storyteller, Jim Johnson. Jim, for a time a pastor in the Evangelical Lutheran Church in America and, along with his wife, Nancy, for a time owner of the Bull 'n Bear Saloon and Casino in Red Lodge, Montana, recounted these stories to me and others many times. They never failed to delight, teach, and inspire. He, finally, agreed to our pleading that he write them down and publish them as this book

Through these stories be prepared to find God, indeed, Jesus Himself by the power of the Holy Spirit, in a bar and casino in a resort town in Montana. Be prepared to hear how God crosses the bar in the everyday lives of regulars and visitors who make their way into conversation with this pastor/bar owner. Be prepared to read how in this bar God crosses the massive gap between death and life, creation and a new creation, hate and love, fear and trust, guilt and forgiveness, and especially shame and honor.

May your reading increase your sense of the power of God to cross the massive divides and obstacles in your life and our society, even the one between the bar people and church people. Whether you are bar people or church people, or both, blessed crossings.

Pat Keifert
Professor of Systematic Theology, Luther Seminary
President and Director of Research, Church Innovations

ACKNOWLEDGEMENTS

Just like a good song fairly begs to be both sung and heard more than once, so it is with expressing thanks to those who have enriched my life by allowing me to walk with them along the road we have traveled. In this case, the song of thanks I want to sing for them is for both those who have journeyed with me as what God was up to became more and more clear as we "crossed the bar," and for those who helped me put the stories of that journey into words. First, however, I want to say a word of thanks for roots.

The lives of my four siblings and I were blessed with parents whom we not only love, but who were good and decent people who loved God and who lived like it. As such, they earned not only our love, but also our respect. Since it is not all that often that one is allowed publicly to express such things, with Steve, Dave, Sharon and Tom, I thank you, Roy and Sophie Johnson, for being nothing more or less than who you are. It couldn't have been better.

Now for my friends in the bar who often joked about walking into a bar only to find that their bartender was a preacher. Over the years, in addition to becoming friends, some of you joined us at a campfire down by the river to wonder together about what God has done and is doing still. Among those at our early Christmas campfires were Jim, Stena Bushnell and their son Maverick, Mencel Carey, my children Ben, Katie and Megan Johnson and Nancy's children Jeni and Aaron Leatherberry. Over the years others joined us as well: Ed Weast, David Tilton, Will Tilton, Bill "about half" Spencer, Kathy Kennedy, Eileen Thebolt, Marsha Keller, Ralph Rehard, Cindy and Bill (Bubba) Smith, Delcy Bulau, Sarah Harvey, Richard and Terri Welbes, Connie and Frank Salo, Micky Thiel, Sue Axton, and Barry and Peggy Smith. Some have become a regular part of our church by the river, others come less frequently, but I thank you all for your trust and for allowing me to be, not only your bartender and not only your preacher, but also your friend.

For over a decade, God's servants at Church Innovations have been involved in the writing of *Crossing the Bar*; in fact, it was for CI that Pat Keifert first asked that I write articles for their newsletter and its readers. CI then followed up this invitation with encouragement, editing, insight, prodding and deadlines—and finally all the support and work that went into turning it all into a book. In this final process I am thankful especially to Barbara Miller, who has been instrumental in getting this thing done. I am grateful and proud to be serving God's mission in the world with such people as make up Church Innovations.

The last two words of thanks I have saved for expressing my deep gratitude to my two best friends: Pat Keifert, and my wife, Nancy Minion.

It is simply a fact that this book would not exist if it were not for Pat Keifert. The first suggestion that I start writing down these stories came from Pat as I talked with him about them on our too-infrequent fishing trips, and he was there every step of the way with insight and understanding (wisdom) that still has me in awe. But as much as I value all that he has done in regard to the writing of this book, it pales in comparison to how I value his friendship. Pat has been my friend through the good and the bad of nearly 30 years, and I could neither ask nor hope for a better or truer friend.

The final word of thanks I owe is to my wife, Nancy. Not only was the writing of each and every one of these stories supported by her, the joys and struggles that each story reveals were lived side by side with her as well. She has been my partner and traveling companion every step of the journey, going to work with me every day to help put bread on the table, encouraging me during those seemingly "meaningless" times, making our house a home to return to every day, and making me deeply grateful to her, and to our Lord and creator, that I am her husband in this world God loves.

❖ Author's Note on Language ❖

In writing a book such as this, it is difficult to draw a balance between not using language that will offend some readers and using the language of the real characters whose stories are being told. It is never my intention to needlessly offend, but sometimes the real words of the characters simply must be used in order to catch the true flavor, and occasionally the irony, of the way things were actually said and done.

As you will soon see, it is my belief that when God came among us in the person of Jesus, he clearly landed right in the middle of people whose language was sometimes rough. It is also clear that this did not dissuade him from being with them, listening to them, healing them and giving them hope, even laughing and celebrating with them in order to accept and love them.

If you are one who will be offended by the occasional use of rough language, I am truly sorry to have offended. I would be sorrier still, however, if my concern to not offend (either in the writing or the living of these stories) ever got in the way of what God is up to in the lives of anyone in this world God so loves.

№ 1 ∞ CHURCH PEOPLE AND BAR PEOPLE: BACK IN THE SADDLE AGAIN 23

№ 2 ∞ WHERE IS JESUS? THOSE SORTS OF PEOPLE AND THOSE SORTS OF PLACES .. 31

№ 3 ∞ HOW CHRISTIANS ARE VIEWED................................. 39

№ 4 ∞ WHAT WAS JESUS FOR? 49

№ 5 ∞ GLIDING 61

№ 6 ∞ MARY-MARY 73

№ 7 ∞ WHEN WISDOM BENDS HER KNEE 85

№ 8 ∞ AN UNNECESSARY GOD 99

№ 9 ∞ KNOWING THE HOUSE YOU PLAY IN 107

№ 10 ∞ A HARD CASE OR HOW TO GET FROM THE CHURCH TO THE BAR . 115

№ 11 ∞ HOME BY ANOTHER WAY 129

№ 12 ∞ THE WONDERFUL PROBLEM OF THE FREEDOM OF GOD 143

№ 13 ∞ "I LOVE THIS BAR!" 153

№ 14 ∞ THE ATTACK OF THE BIBLE THUMPER 163

№ 15 ∞ FREEDOM AND THE CHURCH OF THE ULTIMATE 171

№ 16 ∞ KRISSY, TIGGER, JESUS, AND JAMES DEAN 181

№ 17 ∞ MILK FOR FREE 189

№ 18 ∞ MARVIN'S GARDENS 201

№ 19 ∞ TUMBLING 211

Introduction

...and then the boat I was in went over the falls.

IF YOU HAD TOLD ME when I was fresh out of seminary that I would spend a decade serving as a Lutheran parish pastor—then go on to run a saloon and casino in the same small Montana ski resort town where I had pastored, I would have asked you, "What have you been drinking?"

Yet here I am, about to tell you stories of what turned out to be exactly that life, a life filled with assumptions thrown aside, questions never before considered taking center stage, and deep friendships formed with people I wouldn't have met as a pastor.

Now, when you are a preacher who spends as much time as I have in a bar, especially when *you* are the one serving the drinks, you learn to expect certain questions—and certain reactions after you respond.

"I used to be a Lutheran pastor."

That's what I told people when they asked me from across the bar about what I did before owning and operating Red Lodge, Montana's Bull'n Bear Saloon and Casino with my wife, Nancy.

"A *pastor?!*" they'd invariably exclaim, eyes twinkling with surprise. Then I'd hear the first of two questions:

"What happened?" they would ask, expecting, I suppose, to hear a story they'd probably not heard before.

The second question, however, took me by surprise, and not only when I heard it for the first time, but almost every time thereafter.

"What made you lose your faith?"

Answering the second question was easy.

"I didn't lose my faith," I would respond. "In fact, even though the path has been somewhat perilous at times, I think my faith in God is deeper. At least now I understand some things that I would never have even thought about if I had remained a parish pastor."

"In fact," I would continue, this time with *my* eyes twinkling, "I think going to a bar regularly ought to be required training for pastors! I wonder if I could sign up for 'hazardous duty pay' as a continuing education instructor for the church...."

At this, the patrons would smile and say something like, "As if the church would do something like that!" Then we'd move on.

Answering the first question, however, was usually a little stickier and took considerably longer. But on the slow, wintry evenings when I was pulling the night shift—because we couldn't afford to hire a bartender for more than two or three of the 14 regular shifts—there was plenty of time. Besides, like the question about "losing my faith," that first question almost always led to interesting conversations, regardless of which direction they took. And interesting conversations are part of what running a bar is all about.

Back to that first query: "What happened," I told patrons, "was that I went through a divorce and wasn't in any shape to be the pastor of a parish, at least not for a while. So I resigned and spent a year or two traveling and doing concerts in churches. I am also a musician and songwriter. After that, all in the space of one year, Nancy and I got married, bought this joint, and built a house. And here I am, talking with you."

Now all of this was the truth; it just wasn't the *whole* truth. But people didn't need to know the whole truth, I figured, at least not right away. It really wasn't any of their business.

But if you, the reader, are going to fully understand what you are going to encounter in this book, I need to fill in some blanks. I will do this now by giving you a more complete answer to that first question—and introducing myself to you more completely. (As Kris Kristofferson wrote in "Me and Bobby McGee," "Freedom's just another word for nothing left to lose," and though I didn't view it as much of a blessing at the time, I had—and still have—truly been blessed with such freedom.)

The "whole truth," or at least as much as is pertinent here, is that during the time when I was serving my second parish as a Lutheran pastor, Nancy and I fell in love with one another, while we were both still in other (albeit troubled) marriages. We broke every commandment that goes along with such a situation. (Yes, there are many more commandments than the most obvious one.)

As you might imagine, as I took my trip down that particular "run in the river," I became significantly bruised and battered as I bounced from boulder to rock while being swept along by the terribly unruly rapids created by being a pastor who is trying to be faithful to his calling while having an extramarital affair.

On one hand, I was tossed about by feelings of wondrous elation (feelings that colored how I viewed almost everything and called into question my understanding of life) and terrible guilt on the other hand. Deep inside, I knew that God, whom I love, was the source of wisdom that was foundational to that understanding.

As I was carried away by the raging river my life had become, I desperately tried to grasp the wood of the cross. Over and over, I rushed by it, but it seemed just out of reach.

But as terrible, exhilarating, frightening, and exciting as those waters were, they didn't compare to what happened after Nancy and I were "found out," and the wider church denomination, with its bishops, systems, and need to "set an example," entered the picture.

I should note at this point that I grew up in a faithful Christian home with wonderful parents and in a church with a wise pastor named Pete Waldum. (The late Pastor Waldum is still the best preacher I've ever heard.)

I benefited from years of education at a first-rate seminary before serving as a parish pastor for a decade. My experience and education had shown me that the gospel's prescription for sin (and therefore the church's prescription as well) was repentance and forgiveness. Naively, just as I had trusted and taught this understanding of sin and grace, I assumed that the church would treat me accordingly, even in my present circumstance.

A person sins. He repents and is forgiven. End of story. It is finished.

Or is it?

I soon learned that the church didn't necessarily practice what it preached. And this is a scary revelation when a church holds both your past (who I had come to understand myself to be) and your future in its powerful hands.

For all of my life, I had understood myself to be a sinner in deep need of Christ's forgiveness. This realization was never clearer than when I was unfaithful in my marriage. I became more aware than ever that our need for a savior is not just part of a doctrine of atonement. It's a dire necessity of life for each of us.

I also held tightly to the image that the Church, which I deeply love and which had been born of that forgiveness, was like a ship that not only carried and delivered this most precious cargo of the gospel, but also protected us in tempestuous seas as well.

And then the ship I was in went over the falls.

"Of course your sins, even *this* one, are forgiven by God," my bishop told me as we sat in the parsonage living room, discussing the fallout of my infidelity. "But this has nothing to do with forgiveness."

Up to this point, I had been staring out the picture window, but now my gaze turned to him. I saw him and heard him, but I felt I was in a fog that was deepening by the second. I tried to take in his words. It was hard to do that day, but I would learn just how true his words would turn out to be. *"This has nothing to do with forgiveness."*

To be sure, my official and professional relationship with the church has profoundly and permanently affected my life, but this book isn't about the church's response to a crisis. I've shared this much about my church's response to help you understand my background and reasons for writing this book. This isn't a story of "who did what, and to whom." It's not my autobiography. It's a story of a loving God who works in unexpected ways, in unexpected places.

Suffice it to say that my church was both faithful to and good at proclaiming God's grace and the forgiveness of our sins in Christ. However, it was equally as good at making sure that *shame* remains, especially for "those" sins.

In "Piece of Work," singer/songwriter Jimmy Buffett noted that he is "best known for his worst mistakes."

I understand Jimmy. Even now, more than 20 years after my divorce and remarriage, I sometimes find myself plucked up by someone from the church and placed once again at the edge of the falls, where I'm forced to relive my failures. So that I can avoid forgetting "who I really am."

"And," as Forest Gump was wont to say, "that's all I have to say about that."

There are a couple more things, however, that I wish to touch now on by way of introducing you to *Crossing the Bar*, even though I will deal with them more completely in the stories that follow.

The first is the incredible power of *shame*, especially as it affects those outside the church. I mention it here so you will be sure to look for it as you read the stories, for it lies just beneath the surface in a good number of them.

In all my years of making good friends in the Bull'n Bear and talking with them about the wonder of Christ, who is "God with us," the most common story (after story after story) I have heard centers on the seemingly insurmountable distance they feel between themselves and the church. This distance exists whether someone was once part of a church or has never had a thing to do with organized religion. Shame creates this distance. As you will see, the specter of shame is *huge* for so many people, and the toll it takes on them is inestimable.

When I speak of shame, I don't want you to confuse it with appropriate remorse—those times when we should feel bad for something we've done. That's part of a healthy conscience, the kind of conscience that leads us to seek Jesus and ask His forgiveness.

Rather, the shame I'm talking about is the sense of feeling, not worthless, but *worth less* than others around you, especially if you are a church "outsider." This shame reveals itself in oft made statements like, "The church doesn't want people like me around." It lurks just beneath the surface— so it can't be identified for what it is—but it's there, always ready to do its ungodly damage.

To be sure, our sense of shame often comes from within us. The Talmud, a collection of Jewish wisdom, says that "we do not see things as *they* are; we see things as *we* are."

Often, though, shame is imposed on us from outside, imposed by those who have the power in our lives to make shame stick. The church has this power, and this is one reason many people who were once involved in a church have left.

For me, both internal and external sources contributed to the shame I experienced so strongly—and hated just as strongly.

But my experience also set my feet firmly in a good place. It made me a brother to all those I would meet, people making the same trip I made. The trip from the church to the bar.

My journey has convinced me that the church must deal with this issue of shame. You can't share the joy of the gospel of Jesus with people who feel like they are being judged— that they are unwelcome, unworthy, and unwanted. To put it as plainly as I am able, the church must deal with how it is perceived by outsiders. To them, the message the church has most often given them is, "God accepts you just as you are—as long as you are just like *we* are!"

This leads me to the second "heads-up" I want to give you before you dive into *Crossing the Bar*.

Early in my journey from the church to the bar, I learned that there is a great chasm between how the Christian church views itself and how outsiders view it. One of my goals for this book is to bridge the gap between two worlds that are much more alike than either realizes.

We who are the church are at our best when we see ourselves as people called to carry to the world God's message of love and grace, shown to us in Jesus Christ our Lord. This is the mission of God to which the church has been called.

But this isn't the picture of the church seen by those outside its fellowship. One of our recent U.S. Presidents called the church "the protector of the public morality." Many church-goers would say amen to that definition. But to the typical unchurched person, those words mean that the church is filled with "the ones who want to tell us how to live our lives."

Whether you are part of the Christian church and striving to carry out God's mission in this world, or you are on the "outside" and want to know more about God's love and peace, you will be miles ahead if you acknowledge the vast difference between how outsiders view the church and how the church views itself. Helping to bridge this gap has been an integral part of my role, my calling from God, over the past several years.

Having said that, it's now time to move on and to introduce you to my customers and friends. My boat mates, among whom I have been pleased and proud to pull at the oars.

Sometimes my life still seems so odd to me! For the first 10 years of running the Bull'n Bear, my nightly prayers with Nancy always included this simple plea: "Get us out of here!" Every time I walked through the bar's back door, I felt a double shame: I didn't feel like I belonged in a bar, but I was no longer welcome in my church either. The church my pastor-heart still longed for.

But somewhere along the line, my feelings finally changed. Now I am deeply grateful to God for this most wonderful trip! I simply cannot imagine anything better than the fact that this preacher and his beloved bride of 17 years ended up in a bar! During this unlikely journey, even in the darkest times, God remained at work. And though it took me many years, it is an amazing thing to finally see God lovingly and purposefully working away with whatever is available to work with. He can even work through lives as tossed-about as mine, and perhaps yours as well. For we have all known our share of "unruly rapids."

This is, after all, what God seems to be about in this creation gone awry: Looking for that one sheep lost from His fold, searching for that precious lost coin, or waiting for his child to finally come back home. We are privileged to be invited by God to join the search—*and* the rejoicing and the partying to come, along with the whole host of heaven.

So come on in. Let me pour you a cold one, or just a cup of coffee or tea if you prefer. Let's talk. I'd like you to meet some very good friends of mine, friends I think you will enjoy. All you have to do is cross the bar. We'll go together.

Church People and Bar People:
Back in the Saddle Again

IT HAS BEEN SEVERAL YEARS now since Parker called me one night at the Bull'n Bear Saloon to tell me that his dad had just died.

"He said he was a little tired," Parker explained, "and was going to bed early. He just didn't wake up."

"I'm really sorry," I said. "I liked your dad."

Parker's dad, Art, used to let me and my friends hunt birds on his property. Nancy and I got to know Art pretty well because he and Parker used to stop by the Bull'n Bear and visit when they came to town pick up supplies for their ranch. Parker would have a can of beer, his dad a Mountain Dew. ("I drank enough beer when I was younger to last me," Art explained.)

We'd swap stories (some of them even true), and I always had to stifle a smile when Art laughed, revealing gaps formerly occupied by two prominent bottom teeth. Perhaps all that beer and how it tends to make you say things best left unsaid doomed his teeth one fateful day. More likely, a calf got a hoof free during a branding and lashed out in defense.

"Jim, I was wonderin'..." Parker paused, and then continued, "Well... I don't know any damn preachers...and... well, do you still do funerals? Would you be willing to 'come out of retirement' and do Dad's funeral?"

The question hit me like a load of bricks. My journey from pulpit to bar owner had been, as a friend of mine once put it, through "some rather unruly waters." I was still pretty wet and banged up from it all.

"Parker, I haven't done a funeral for over five years now."

"I know that. It's just that Dad liked you, and...."

"I'd be honored to," I offered, sensing his discomfort. I didn't tell him that I'd be scared to death as well. *Crossing back over from the bar to the pulpit?* I thought, closing my eyes. I didn't need this. My own faith, while not lost, was hard for me then—*really* hard. And willingly re-entering churning waters, and encountering certain "church people," seemed like an act of masochism.

Nevertheless, four days later I helped lay Art to rest. During the funeral, I talked with his friends and family about God, who created them and loves them. God, who remains faithful to His promises, even though we, like myriad other characters who fill the pages of Scripture, have often been unfaithful. And as I preached for the first time in several years, I experienced something rare: The whole room full of people, most of whom had seldom, if ever, darkened the door of a church, sat still and attentive. Some even leaned forward! All were listening hard to what I was saying about Art, God, and Art-and-God. It was as if they had never heard such words before.

Right now I'm not going to recite exactly what I said at Art's funeral, or describe what happened after the service. That will come later. Suffice it to say that like a puppy a few weeks after its birth, my eyes started to open, just a little bit. And that experience served to water a seed that had been planted years before, when Nancy and I first took over the Bull'n Bear and hosted the retirement party for Dunbar, the fellow who sold us the bar.

Here is that story.

For several years, a woman named Linda tended bar at the Bull'n Bear for Dunbar, and she had agreed to continue working for us. She was, as the song goes, "a friendly gal," kind-hearted and quick with a wink or a laugh.

But at the retirement party, at least with me, she was different.

As I carried my cup of coffee out into the crowd to meet people, as I had done for years during church "fellowship hours," Linda grabbed my arm, pulled me behind the bar, and admonished, "You can't go out there with *coffee*! Good Lord! People are going to have a hard enough time trusting you because you were a preacher!" She grabbed a bottle of whiskey and poured me a "real drink."

"You may as well learn one thing right now," she then continued. "There are *church* people, and there are *bar* people. The church people don't want us in their churches, and we sure as hell don't want them around here, telling us what to do!"

Even after all I had been through with church people, I wanted to take exception to Linda's conclusion. It offended my view of what the church was about. But I thought better and kept my mouth shut, which was absolutely the right thing to do. Because when you consider how the church interacts with many local communities, Linda was right on target. I have become dear friends with many "bar people," and most in the church would be shocked if they knew how those outside the church really view them. (More on that later.)

By the way, I obeyed Linda that day. I dutifully took my whiskey in hand and joined the company of bar patrons, a stranger in a foreign land.

The retirement party and Art's funeral occurred years apart, but these events—and many others—have profoundly affected how I try to live as a Christian in contemporary culture.

My eyes were opened, and what did I see?

Two things.

1) Our towns and neighborhoods are filled with people who are unlikely to be reached with the gospel via a preacher—because preachers are perceived as being too "other." (By the way, I refer to these folks as bar people, but many of them don't frequent bars. They could just as well be called the unchurched.)

2) The overwhelming majority of church people could (and probably *would*) connect with bar people—if only the church encouraged and instructed them on how to make the connections without making everyone involved feel awkward and uncomfortable. (This instruction, for example, would help church people understand that they won't burst into flames if they step foot in a bar.)

When I used the term "overwhelming majority of church people," in the paragraph above, I wasn't exaggerating. You do not have to attend the pastor's advanced Bible study or be a member of a church council to be equipped to take the gospel to bar people. This task isn't for the "super-faithful few."

In fact, the rank-and-file parishioners might be better poised to go boldly (or gently) to places a pastor or deacon cannot or will not go.

Why?

First, the average Joe and Joanne in the pew are less likely to have an identity so tied up in their congregation and/or denomination that there is little contact with the world beyond. Many churches provide "fellowship groups," "supper clubs," softball teams, long-term craft projects, youth programs, and sports leagues for the kids. And this is all in addition to worship services, Sunday school, and Bible studies. If you know a zealous family who rarely participates in any activity that *isn't* connected to their church, then you understand what I'm talking about.

Second, because as the Average Joe and Joanne "cross the bar" in their everyday lives, they don't view themselves as "church people." They're just regular people who happen to attend church. And regular people are often as comfortable mingling with bar people as they are with other members of their church.

These folks follow the example of Jesus, who was known as (and *criticized as*) "a friend of sinners." You are just as likely to find them sitting on a bar stool as in a pew. And when I say bar stool, I am not necessarily only being literal.

I am talking also about the "bar stools of life": On the job at a secular company. Shopping at the mall. Hunting or fishing with buddies from college or their job.

Their world transcends church boundaries. They sometimes tell jokes that are less than tasteful, less than politically correct. They fit in with people beyond the church, and they often do so without the church's encouragement—sometimes without even so much as the church's approval.

Sometimes, these followers of Christ find themselves in the situation of helping their friends sort out what God is up to, what it all means. This often happens when a "bar friend" has to see a loved one buried. These are moments when God's "other sheep" hunger for the ministry of His rank-and-file sons and daughters—not necessarily a pastor or other well-heeled church professional.

This is what "crossing the bar" is all about. Joining God's work-a-day mission, just as Jesus did. Blessing others by our presence and our occasionally unpolished words. Shining a bit of light in a dark room. Engaging (rather than avoiding) the kind of people Jesus engaged, laughed with, and showed compassion to.

There is a beautiful old Finnish hymn called "Lost in the Night," which portrays God's mission in the world. This hymn is powerful because it is written from the perspective of those who do not yet know God—the bar people—but feel the need to:

"Must we be vainly awaiting the morrow?
Will those who have light no light let us borrow?
Giving no heed to our burden of sorrow?

Will you help us soon? Will you help us soon?"

We have the Word, which is for all people. We have women, men, and young people who are in exactly the right places to reach out to the bar people in their lives. What is left, but to encourage, to bless, and to send?

What is left but to cross the bar?

WHERE IS JESUS?
(THOSE SORTS OF PEOPLE &
THOSE SORTS OF PLACES)

AFTER I HAD OPERATED the Bull'n Bear for a few years, a joke started to circulate around Red Lodge: "Two guys walked into a bar and stopped in their tracks. One thought to himself, *Oh no, my preacher's a bartender!* The other thought, *Oh no! My bartender's a* preacher!

I first heard that joke about eight years ago, but something that happened a few nights ago brought it to mind again. It was one of those slow, off-season nights, and there were only three people in the Bull'n Bear. Then a lone woman walked in, ordered a cup of coffee, and retreated to the "buddy bar" by the front window. She sat there, looking out the window into the dark night. She accepted refill after refill, downing cup after cup of bar coffee until well after midnight.

She looks so sad, I thought. I wondered if I should say something to her, but chose not to. That's something a preacher learns when he becomes a bartender: Sometimes people just want to be left alone.

As the clock moved toward 1 a.m., my three previous customers filed out. I made my way to the buddy bar and offered the woman another refill. She turned to me and said, "You wouldn't by any chance know where I could find a pastor to talk to at this time of night, would you?" I smiled a little smile. "Just a minute," I said. "I'll get us *both* some fresh coffee."

I poured two cups and told her that I was a Lutheran pastor who had served a local parish for several years.

Her face showed both relief and anxiety. "My bartender's a preacher?" she said.

This encounter raises a couple important questions for we who are serious about bringing God's good love into the lives of people we're unlikely to see in the pews on Sunday.

The questions . . .

If we truly believe in the wonder and joy of the Incarnation—of "God with us" through Christ—just where do we expect to find Jesus among us today?

Moreover, if we who are believers in and disciples of Jesus are, in St. Paul's words, "the body of Christ, and individually members of it," just where do we expect to *take* Jesus?

Or, to push the point even further, such questions might be more easily answered if we turn them over and look at their flipsides: Are there places we do *not* expect to find Jesus? Are there places we've been told we shouldn't take Him?

Now, our knee-jerk reaction might be simple and expected:" "Christ is *everywhere!*" we say. Which is, of course, true. "We ought to take Jesus *wherever* we go!" (That's true too—though the waters become more troubled a little farther downstream, when we realize that indeed we *do* take Him wherever we go, for better or for worse, whether we intend to or not!)

But if we were to look around with eyes willing to see beyond our own little "sanctuaries," we would realize that these answers, while they may seem self-evident to us, are not what we convey to those outside the Christian church, those who have not experienced the gospel we hold so dear.

The way we "do church," how we embody God's mission as we share our faith (or comment publicly about social issues) speaks volumes to those outside the church. It conveys who we really are and what we really believe. The same can be said about the times we choose *not* to share our faith or speak out on an issue.

Who of us hasn't experienced those times—such as walking into a bar—when we feel like we should hang up Jesus at the entryway, along with our hats and coats. Then we can reclaim Him later, on our way out the door.

Ironically, shortly after writing this chapter, a woman walked into the Bull'n Bear and shared this quote from her pastor's recent sermon: "Don't you take Jesus into a bar and put Him in front of all that liquor!"

Today's "media Christians" sing the same kind of song, even more loudly. Imagine your perspective on the gospel of Jesus if it were based solely on what you heard from TV preachers. Yet this is reality for many of those outside the church. For the bar people. They have a clear picture of what the church believes, but it's the wrong picture.

They've come to believe that Jesus and "those sorts of people" don't mix. Jesus doesn't belong in "those sorts of places." Never mind that Jesus came to earth to engage people as they are, and where they are.

(A brief aside: I learned early in my dubious career as a bar owner that bar people often have a better understanding than church people of what the church *should* be in contemporary society. Churches talk about bringing the righteousness, love, and peace of our Lord to those who haven't experienced them. But what they say and how they operate are in stark contrast. We need to better understand how "they" see us. Otherwise, we will continue to find ourselves saying one thing while "they" hear quite another!)

How, exactly, do bar people see church people?

They see us as judges, critics who want to tell them how to live, rather than telling them God has given His life for us all. (Remember Linda's comment from Chapter 1: ". . . and we sure don't want the church people in the bar, telling us what to do!")?

Bar people see us wanting to change them into church people—so that they'll be acceptable to God. Or to say it another way, they believe that church people want to "circumcise" their lives so that they'll look the part.

This brings us back to the questions from earlier in this chapter.

Where do we expect to find Jesus, we who have heard the good news and live in its promise?

The immediate answer for many of us, certainly me, too, is, "We find Jesus in the Word and Sacraments," where He promised He would be present. Jesus' presence here is mysterious, but it's not "hocus pocus," as one of my patrons recently put it. It's very real and important to me and many of my fellow believers. In much the same way as God spoke in creation "and it was so," Jesus said He would be there, and so He is.

But are there other places where Jesus is to be found, besides the Word and the Sacraments?

The Lord is in His creation, of course. A lot of my bar friends, especially the ranchers, seek God in nature. And while God does reveal much about Himself in creation, that's not the whole story. They fail to see that God doesn't' just *reveal* Himself in creation. He entered into creation to restore humanity and have a personal relationship with men, women, and children. Missing this part of the story results in an image of a God who is a powerful creative being, but not much more.

This viewpoint also misses the truth that Jesus can be found in the poor and down-trodden. He said we would find Him there. He said we would find Him among those in prison and among the hungry and sick and lonely. You can find the whole list in Matthew 25.

During the past few years, I've begun to wonder if there's yet another "place" we should expect to find Jesus—a place we have forgotten about, or failed to consider at all.

This is the place (places, really) where Jesus Himself "crossed the bar." Places He visited intentionally, despite the criticism of the Pharisees. Places right in His neighborhood (and ours as well).

I'm talking about the places where the lost are to be found: ("I came to seek and save the lost," Jesus said. See Luke 15: 3-10.) That's why He went where the "sick" and the "sinners" were. ("Those who are well do not need a physician, but those who are sick," He proclaimed. "I came not to call the righteous, but sinners." Mark 2:17).

And when Jesus found the people he sought, He ate and drank with them, even though He was harshly criticized for it. ("He eats and drinks with sinners!" Luke 15:2). He went to "those sorts of places" and cared about "those sorts of people," touching their hearts and lives. (Remember the woman who was so affected by Jesus that she washed His feet with her tears and wiped them dry with her hair—while a "church person," a Pharisee, looked on, saying, "Doesn't he know what sort of woman it is that is touching him!" Luke 7:39). Like it or not, that's who Jesus is. He's not the kind of shepherd who focuses on the sheep that are fattened up and handsomely groomed for the county fair. He is the shepherd who goes looking for the un-groomed lost lamb as well.

So what's the point of all this?

Just this: I believe that a sad, coffee-drinking woman sitting in my bar late one night found Jesus there for her, through me. At least *she* thought so. And she found Him in a most unexpected place.

Some church people will proclaim, "Don't go taking Jesus into that bar!" but that's where Jesus *was* for one woman. There in a bar, amid all that liquor. And I am thankful for that. I have sat at a window like that a few times in my life as well, hoping for a sign that God cares about me.

Truth be told, everyone experiences moments like this. Bar people and church people alike, both longing for a sense of God's presence, God's direction.

God comes to us personally, and what better way to connect personally than through an actual person?

I don't discount that God can make himself known in many ways, but it seems that almost always He chooses to reach out to us through His children. And sometimes these connections seem to come about by pure happenstance.

This is why this chapter's questions matter so much. Imagine what can happen when the church finally "gets it!" Jesus is eager to accompany us to "those places," the places He frequented, seeking and saving. Eating and drinking. Healing, touching, and being touched—by "those sorts of people." The not-ready-for-county-fair sheep who have either wandered far from the Good Shepherd or have never known that there even was a Good Shepherd looking for them that He might care for them as well.

It's important to note again that you don't have to be a superstar church member to cross the bar. You don't have to be one of the "show-ready" sheep to be part of this mission. You never know when one of your friends might be "sitting by the window" of life, needing to meet the Jesus you know well. You don't have to memorize a speech or a bunch of doctrine. You can start by simply saying something like, "I know that I haven't talked about this much, but maybe it would help if I told you about something that has helped me when I was sitting where you are now."

Jesus was not your typical "church person." I think we all agree on that. He wasn't your typical "bar person" either, so let's not fall off the other side of the theological horse.

He was "God with us." God with *all* of us, who did not limit then (or now) where, or with whom, He might be found. His gifts of healing, peace, and saving love are for all sorts of people, in all sorts of places.

What would happen if the people who regularly (or occasionally) cross the bar understood that they didn't need to check Jesus at the door, along with their hats and coats? That they didn't need to be embarrassed or self-conscious about bringing their Lord with them wherever they went?

What would happen if the people who took this Jesus who matters *to* them, *with* them?

My bet is that more bar people would get to know a God who is *with* them, and not simply some church people who are perceived as being against them.

How Christians Are Viewed

Grace is our resident "church lady." For years, she's served our small congregation faithfully (though sometimes, it has seemed, also resentfully). One day, she showed up at the bar with a year's supply of offering envelopes for me. Because, I suppose, they were "church stuff" and she didn't want to embarrass me, she had wrapped them in a plain brown paper bag, taped shut.

THIS PAST EASTER, after a lovely day together, Nancy and I walked down the path behind our home to Rock Creek, which borders our property. There we built an evening campfire and watched as the water hurried toward us, and then rushed away again, not unlike a lot of things in life. We commented that many people have to walk several hard, rocky miles to reach a place like this. But it's practically in our backyard. We are most truly blessed.

Sitting there before the campfire, my mind turned toward my dad, who had died nearly four years earlier. In the midst of missing him, mixed with the peace that comes from the hope in the promise of resurrection, I remembered an unusual woman who had come into the Bull'n Bear several years earlier—long before Dad died. After a little barroom chat, and several double Grey Goose vodka-and-cranberry drinks, she suddenly asked, "When you die, how do you want to be remembered by your children?" Not your typical barroom question. I thought for a moment before replying: "If my kids remember me the same way I remember my dad, it'll be all right with me." Again, I am truly blessed. There are far too many people who could not or would not say the same thing.

After "adjusting" that Easter fire for a while (as those who sit at a campfire are wont to do), Nancy and I read the post-Crucifixion and Resurrection account (from John's gospel) of Peter and the rest of the guys sitting by their fire on the beach, apparently not knowing what to do with themselves, given all that had recently taken place. (Before we read the passage, I had told Nancy it was my favorite of the Resurrection stories, and as soon as Peter got up, muttering the words "I'm going fishing," her smile flashed an understanding of my fondness for this text.)

When we finished reading the story, we laughed at what Peter and his fishing buddies must have thought (the same thing I would have thought) when someone came along, asking how the fishing was going—while they were deep in the middle of "getting skunked."

I could only imagine someone asking this of me and my fishing buddy Pat—and then having the gall to suggest we might do better by "throwing out on the other side of the boat."

As I write this chapter, I can almost see Pat, peering over his sunglasses at me in annoyance with this intruder and his ill-timed and ill-advised suggestion. Then I can imagine the surprise in those same eyes as we start hauling 'em in. More fish than we could dream of. More than we'd even dare lie about (if we told such lies). And if we had been there with Peter, you'd have to add into the mix the utter amazement at our crucified and formerly dead Lord, fixing us a bite to eat there on the beach, full of the life of God, completing a fishing story that was absolutely unbelievable but obviously and undeniably true; a story crying out to be retold.

Not only was Jesus, who was once dead, now alive, the disciples must have thought, but in conquering His death, He has utterly destroyed *our* death as well. Loved ones we thought were forever lost are now loved ones waiting with us for *our* resurrection from the dead, when we will all be together once again. And our hearts, always wanting something more, are finally satisfied, because God has provided what He has wanted for us from the dawn of creation.

These were the things I thought about as Nancy and I watched the rushing creek. That most wonderful news and all that it means lingered in my mind, like so many wisps of smoke in the early evening air, leaving me so thankful that there were people like John, who had not only told us what God has done, but also sought to explain what it means.

These blessings, however, are not what most bar people think of when they ponder what the church is all about. They often hear a "different gospel." For these folks, the church is about something entirely different. The good news the church celebrates at Easter is not the message they hear—or at least hear most loudly.

You've probably heard the story about the guy who walks into a bar and sits down next to a fellow who has a dog sleeping at the foot of his bar stool.

"Does your dog bite?" the new customer asks his fellow patron.

"Nope," the fellow responds. But when the newcomer reaches down to pet the dog, it nearly takes his hand off.

"Hey," the bite victim shouts angrily, "I thought you told me your dog doesn't bite!"

"He doesn't," comes the reply. "That's not my dog."

I have preached many times at funerals of friends who had no relationship with anything "church." And I have been struck by how intently so many attendees listened to my words about the hope God has given us through Christ. No fidgeting. People leaning forward in their seats, striving to catch every word. That kind of listening.

At the first few of these funerals, I truly feared that I would, ironically, bore people to death. But as I talked with various mourners later on, I realized that many of them had simply never heard this stuff before. Or at least not in terms they could understand.

No one had told them, as unimaginable as it may seem, that the God who created us has remained involved in His creation—to the point of taking on flesh Himself to come and win us back after we had wandered away. It was as if the message, if it had been brought to them before, had been delivered in a plain brown paper bag—taped shut, not unlike those offering envelopes from Grace.

Not everyone has a mom or dad to tell him or her about God's promises, or even so much as read about the baby Jesus at Christmas time. Not everyone has gone to Sunday School or had a teacher like my Mrs. Rose to share stories about Jesus. Such as the time when He wanders off in the big city, scaring His parents to death—until they find Him days later, amazing the people in the temple with His insightful understanding of God's promises and purposes.

Or about this Jesus who grew to manhood, healed the sick, raised the dead, and brought good news to the poor and heavily burdened.

Who was put to death on the cross, only to be raised by God from the dead three days later.

Many people don't have pastors to tell them about Jesus and Peter and his fishing partners and their Easter sharing of campfire-cooked fish, as my pastor Pete Waldum did. No one has told these folks that, like Jesus, we too will be raised from our graves—and reunited in heaven with loved ones.

They don't have friends who share why Jesus matters to them in their work-a-day lives.

If people don't have these blessings, how are they to learn what God has done for them through His son Jesus?

All of which brings me back to the joke about the dog.

For most of the people I deal with at the Bull'n Bear, Christianity is not about the hope of a God who seeks us out. The poignancy of Good Friday or the joy of Easter. The freedom from sin and death. No, to them, the church is another kind of dog, a dog that bites.

For many people, their exposure to a church and a pastor is limited to weddings and funerals, both events with profound personal impact.

I am sad to say that most pastors I knew when I was serving a parish simply hated doing such ceremonies for people who weren't "members." "It is simply a waste of time," they grumbled. They were busy enough watching over their own flocks to be bothered with people who didn't share their faith. (Never mind that many of these people had never been told about this faith). Now, if a pastor presided over a funeral with this attitude (one even told me he didn't like to "prostitute our calling" by doing such services), do you think the bar people in attendance just might detect it?

Combine such personal experiences with the "anti-whatever" comments of news-making "Christian personalities" and TV preachers and the picture that develops isn't a pretty one.

Perhaps you remember this: A few days after the September 11 terrorist attacks, one well known television preacher appeared on the television show of an equally well known preacher. On that show, the first told a nationwide audience that the attacks showed that God's "divine protection" had been lifted from the United States because of "abortionists, homosexuals, the American Civil Liberties Union, People for the American Way, internet pornography," and the like. He suggested that God was giving us what we deserved because of our sin. He then pointed his finger at the camera, "in the face" of the aforementioned transgressors and proclaimed, "You caused this." The other responded, "I feel the same way."

Local media coverage often reveals a similar attitude. When a local congregation makes news, it's often because it has decided to speak out against or protest someone or something: gambling, drinking, smoking, sex outside of marriage, etc. (They tacitly proclaim the message my bar friends attribute to them: "We don't drink, and we don't chew, and we don't go with those who do!").

Sometimes, these Christians advocate "sin taxing" the lifestyles of those who drink or chew, gamble or smoke. The clear message is that they seek to change (or, at least, to penalize) the daily lives of all who don't share their values.

A Kansas-based church often protests at the funerals of fallen U.S. military men and women, using these sad occasions to attack gays in the military and gay people in general.

Is it any wonder, then, that when bar people discuss what Christians are all about, they share my bartender Linda's philosophy: "There are church people, and there are bar people. The church people don't want us in their churches, and we sure as hell don't want them around here, telling us what to do!"

Is this the crux of the gospel?

When we come to grips with how outsiders see the church, it's easy to understand why weddings and funerals are incredibly important settings for accomplishing God's mission. When else do people who so severely misunderstand the church show up, willing to listen? If only we will tell them the truth about God's grace.

Weddings and funerals should not be viewed as times when a pastor "prostitutes the calling." Far from it. A funeral can be a "God moment," when the Holy Spirit moves a pastor to tell the simple truth of what God has done for *all* people.

Sharing the true gospel, of course, shouldn't be left only to professional ministers. The church needs to encourage and equip its bar-frequenting, back-pew-sitting members to share what the gospel means to them—using their own life stories. Because one never knows when someone with zero interest in the church might suddenly become open, even eager, to hear the Good News and the hope it brings.

Who better to tell the gospel story than those whose lives have been blessed by it?

Which brings us back, once again, to that Easter evening long ago.

What did Jesus say to Peter and the other disciples while they were out in their boat fishing?

Wasn't it, "Throw your nets out the other side of the boat"?

The disciples' negative reaction to the advice should give us cause for reflection. Assuming that Jesus knew what He was talking about (and He is, after all, God incarnate), how is it that His closest followers seemed to view His advice as ill-advised, untimely, and simply a waste of time? Do we often respond similarly today?

The well-concealed contents of that securely sealed bag delivered by our "church lady" were tools to help me share with others the riches that I, by God's grace, had been given. But the bar people present that day didn't get to see that.

The envelopes were in a plain brown paper bag, taped shut, so only those of us from the church would know what was really inside.

WHAT WAS JESUS FOR?

*Speaking at Clint's funeral, the pastor said, "When it takes
you a long time to die, as it did with Clint, you have time
to think about a lot of things. Things like 'Am I good enough
to get to heaven when I die?' and 'What will God do with me?'
"Well I'm here to tell you," the pastor continued, looking at
Clint's coffin and nodding her head slowly, "Clint, you were
good enough. You were good enough." I leaned toward my
wife and whispered in her ear, "So what was Jesus for?"*

"WHAT WAS THE QUESTION?"

I guess I'm just a slow study. It took me many years of
owning a saloon to figure out what "the question" was. I am
still working on the answer.

Let me explain: My Lutheran heritage gave me assumptions about life on earth and eternal life with God. These
assumptions have informed everything I am.

The most basic of these assumptions is that God created
me to be one way, yet I am another way. That is, I am a sinner.
This fact leaves me in dire need of God's grace, which (like
everything else that's good) God has provided.

It took me a long time to figure out that there was a question behind this assumption. Partly because I thought *everyone* shared the assumption that "the wages of sin is death," and we therefore need a savior.

I was wrong. Not everyone assumes this. It's not even close.

Though it was some 20 years ago now, I'll never forget performing a wedding for Jack, an employer and friend of one of my brothers.

Typically, I invested significant time counseling an engaged couple and preparing them for a new chapter in their lives. However, as a favor to my brother, I agreed to do Jack's wedding on short notice. (The fact that the ceremony was being held in beautiful Jackson Hole, Wyoming, might have influenced my decision as well.)

On the wedding day, I ate lunch with Jack and his fiancée at some swanky outdoor restaurant. As we talked, I soon learned that while this was his bride's first marriage, it was the fifth for 40-something Jack.

I thought of the biblical woman at the well, and plowed on.

When I asked if the couple had any questions about the wedding, the bride had nothing to say. Jack, however, had one question.

"You're not going to refer to us as sinners, are you?" he asked. "Because I'm not one. Neither was my mother."

I was a bit surprised to learn this. My thoughts turned to Jesus and His talk with that woman over a drink from the well, and also to Mary, the mother of our Lord. Until moments before, I had believed *she* was the only mother of a sinless son.

I looked at Jack's bride, felt a stir of compassion, and finished my lunch. Later, I performed the wedding—figuring it was the lesser of two evils. (As I have told you, I am a sinner.) During the 200-mile drive home, I found myself shaking my head, as if to clear it of cobwebs. I felt I had failed somehow, failed Jack and his new bride, and failed my calling. Failure is an effective teacher, but a harsh one too.

For a long time after that wedding, I regarded Jack as a remarkably arrogant person. He was rich and successful. And he had a lovely new wife. It seemed that he was insulated from life's harsh realities.

More recently, however, I have discovered that my view of Jack was rather arrogant of *me*. After all, why should Jack (or his mother) be expected to view life the way I do?

Years' worth of days and nights at the Bull'n Bear have brought me into contact with people for whom guilt seems a non-issue, at least not before God. Most of them see themselves and God through the same lens as that pastor at Clint's funeral.

They believe that when the heavenly scales are loaded up with their good and bad deeds, things will tilt in favor of "good enough." And if you are "good enough," what need is there for a savior?

They don't need to escape God's judgment, they reason, because a fair-minded God will let 'em into heaven because their good outweighs their bad. Never mind what the Bible says, because it holds no more authority for most of them than any other religious book. (As my friend Eddie is fond of telling people, "The Bible was written by a bunch of guys sitting around in robes and drinking beer in some cold castle." Then, pointing to me, he will add, "Hell, Jim here was a preacher, and he doesn't even know who wrote the damn-fool book. He thinks God did."

Do you see the problem? Sin and judgment aren't an issue for my friends at the bar. Or for people like Jack. They perceive no deep need for Jesus, so why would anything we have to say about Him matter?

Unfortunately, that's the wrong question.

Of course people need Jesus. Deep down, many of them feel that need. They just understand it (and express it) differently than many of us church people do.

The bar people's need for Jesus often manifests itself as remorse. Not remorse in the form of guilt over sinning against God, but as a deep sense that they are not the kind of people they could be, or should be. This failure has hurt them and those they love. Bar people describe remorse the same way they describe their regret over a failed marriage or a child who has gone astray.

This remorse has little to do with a fear of God's judgment. They reason, *God is just as fair as I am. I wouldn't sentence myself or anyone else to _eternal_ punishment, so why would I believe that a just and loving God would do that?*

Were I to ask these folks about sin and judgment, they'd look at me like cows trying to figure out a new gate. But if I talk with them about a sense of regret over who they are—versus who they want to be—they lean forward and listen.

The same thing happens when I talk with someone about a loved one who has just died which created in them a deep sense of loss and a lack of hope.

Bar people don't ask the same "ultimate questions" that church people do at these crucial life moments, but the questions they ask nevertheless spring from the core of who they are and who God created them to be, just as it does with church people.

There are a few, of course, who would sing proudly with Frank Sinatra "I did it my way," or agree with the final verses of the poem "Invictus": "I am the master of my fate, I am the captain of my soul." But most simply muddle through life, wishing it were different. They don't understand that the sense of loss they feel may well be the absence of God in their lives. That, apart from Him, we will always feel incomplete.

Some have a sense of God the *Creator,* but their viewpoint on sin and its wages blocks their view regarding their need of God the Savior.

Perhaps this reveals why the church has failed at reaching into the lives of bar people with the gospel. Bar people believe that church people are concerned mainly with how to behave, how to *live.* Too little attention has been given to helping bar people understand who they *are* as children of a God who loves them.

I have come to believe, then, that the way into these people's hearts with the gospel is *not* through emphasizing God's requirements regarding what they *do* (for this is how they interpret anything said about "sin"), but rather by explaining God's perspective on *who and why they are.* Who their Creator who loves them intends them to be. And what difference it makes that they are alive, not just to them, but to God.

These explanations would touch their real needs—needs that most bar people acknowledge. As St. Augustine noted, "Our hearts are restless until they find their rest in God." At first, bar people might not see a need for the forgiveness of sinful deeds, but most do sense that they were meant to be something, something they are not.

This sense of regret and loss is deeply spiritual, even for people who don't describe themselves as spiritual. They are looking for a place to belong, a place where they matter. They need to be shown that the gift of God's grace and reconciliation through Christ will bring them the peace and purpose they crave, even if they don't understand that craving.

I have wondered for a long time about how to best tell the story of God, who wants to reconcile humanity to Himself, in a way that connects with people who hold no assumptions about the universal need for Jesus. I have come to believe that the answer lies in speaking forgiveness and reconciliation—but not hammering on the specific sins one has committed. The focus needs to be not on what we do, but on the chasm between who we *are* and who God intends us to be.

Please understand: In no way do I want to preach "a different gospel." I want no part of the growing "No-Fault God" movement. I do not view God as sitting back in His overstuffed chair, patting His children on the head and cooing, "You're good enough just the way you are." Whenever

I hear this viewpoint being expressed, it brings me back to the question I whispered at Clint's funeral: "Then what was Jesus for?"

Here's where I have landed:

Once there was a rancher who had two boys, John and Jake, who worked the ranch with him. According to local custom, John, the elder brother, would inherit the ranch when the father died. Jake would receive the other assets from the estate. Because of this custom, the oldest brother in a given family was usually the most responsible in the way he lived. His future livelihood would depend on a well-run ranch, as would the family name. The younger siblings, on the other hand, were often more footloose and fancy free.

John and Jake were no exceptions. One day out in the field, Jake approached his dad. "I've been thinking," he said, "when you're gone and John takes over the ranch, I'm gonna have to get another job, and that's okay. But it means that I won't have the freedom to go do things I want to do. So I was wondering . . . what would you think about me taking some money out of the ranch fund—whatever would be mine anyway someday—and getting a head start on things? Maybe I'll be able to find a good job in the city, but if I don't, at least I can go have some fun before I get tied down."

Jake's dad took off his cap and wiped his brow. He looked at his son. "Jake, I've raised you to be a man," he said. "I guess I need to let you make man decisions. I'm not so sure about this, but knowing you, if I don't say yes now, you'll find a way to grind me down till I say yes later on. Your mom and

I will figure out what you've got coming. I just hope you'll be careful, son."

And so off Jake went, his mother, brother, and dad watching the cloud of dust behind his car as he left for the city.

It didn't take Jake long before he knew he was in over his head. City folk have myriad ways to separate a country boy from his money. Soon Jake was broke and looking for any job he could find. Eventually, all the decent jobs dried up, and the once-proud country man found himself scraping and washing plates in an all-night greasy spoon. He was so hungry and broke that he subsisted on leftover scraps that he'd wolf down when no one was looking. Jake was totally ashamed at what he'd become—and of what had become of his grand plans for his life.

Early in his adventure, Jake had phoned home often, telling exciting tales of life in the big city. But as city life humbled him, the calls dwindled. As the months wore on, Jake's family lost track of him because he moved and didn't tell them where he had gone. They didn't know what had happened to him, even if he was still alive.

One day, Jake's boss caught him eating a piece of meat that a customer had spit out because it was too tough. The sight so disgusted his boss that he fired him on the spot.

Jake felt disgusted too. Disgusted and ashamed. Every fiber in his body simply wanted to go back home where he belonged. He had shamefully squandered his inheritance but thought, *maybe if I can come up with just the right words, I can at least sign on as a hired hand back at the ranch.* He would do any job. At least he could taste his mom's cooking again.

On a bus for home, Jake practiced his speech: "Dad, I lost all that money from the ranch fund. I was such a fool, and I know that I'm not who you raised me to be. I'm not asking you to take me back as though nothing's happened, but do ya think I could come back and work for you and John? I'd work hard; I promise you. I don't have anywhere else to go."

When the bus let him off on the highway by the ranch's mailbox, about a mile from the house, Jake started walking, practicing and practicing the speech.

About a half mile out, his mom saw him coming and ran to get John and her husband.

"Jake's home!" she cried. "It's Jake!"

Jake's dad jumped in the pickup and fairly tore up the road on the way to his son. He slammed on the brakes so hard that the pickup nearly skidded sideways. He threw open the door and ran to embrace his son.

"Jacob, I thought you were dead," he said, through the first tears Jake had ever seen him cry. Jake pushed him away a little so that he could make his plea.

"Dad," he stammered through his own tears, "I lost all that money…I know I'm not who you raised me to be. Could I…, uh, job?"

But Jake's dad would have none of this. He barely heard his son's fumbled words.

All of the things Jake thought would be important to his dad—the wasted money, the partying, the soiling of the proud family name—none of them seemed to matter at all.

For the old rancher, his boy was home where he belonged. Their broken relationship was restored. That's all he had ever wanted.

If Jake's father had any say in the matter (and he had *all* the say) the theme of the day was not to be guilt or shame over what his younger son had done. This day was all about joy. Joy over a wayward son's returning to his father's loving arms. Back where he belonged.

Somehow, we who are the church have given the impression to those outside the church that the No. 1 issue that concerns us, and God, is that we have "sinned against heaven and against you, and are not worthy." This, of course, is true, but our understanding of what those words truly mean has been way too limited.

The blunt message that people are unworthy sinners just doesn't penetrate most human hearts. It might resonate within some in the church, but for the bar people, it's not where they live.

If we talk with bar people, however, about the way to go home, about being God's children—welcomed back into His presence where we belong, where we were created to be—things change. If we help them understand that people simply won't feel whole until their relationship with God is restored—and that Jesus came to lead us "back home—this message will reach them.

Here's why: While they (like Jack, he of the five marriages) may not identify or describe themselves as "sinners," they certainly understand what their lives are like because of their sin. Jack didn't identify himself as a sinner, but it doesn't take much of a stretch to know he had to wonder once in a while why a 40-something man was on his fifth marriage.

Deep down, people like Jack understand that they have wandered far from where their Creator meant them to be. They can look at their lives and see: *This isn't what I want for my life, and it's not what God wants either.* And once someone has come to this understanding, my experience has been that he or she will *welcome* someone showing the way back home.

It may be "home by another way," but it's still coming home. Home where we all belong.

GLIDING

EDDIE, WHOM YOU MET BRIEFLY in the previous chapter, is a farmer and rancher who reads voraciously and stays too long at the watering hole when he comes into town. He's also my friend.

For years I have pondered what, if anything, has authority in the lives of unchurched—even anti-church—people like Eddie.

For me, authority comes from my church's traditional confessions, such as, "The Bible is the sole authority for all matters of faith and life." This is what I was taught, and I've believed it ever since my mom and dad introduced me to "Jesus loves me, this I know, for the Bible tells me so."

For Eddie, though, the Bible holds zero authority. He won't believe something merely because the Bible proclaims it. He has no basis for trusting Scripture. I suppose that that's why God put a guy like me across the bar from a guy like him.

One of Ed's favorite things to do while perched on his favorite stool at the Bull'n Bear (the fourth stool from the end, just opposite the triple sinks) is to introduce me to newcomers, using a line similar to the one from Chapter 4: "Jim here used to be a preacher, but he doesn't even know who wrote the damn-fool Bible. I keep telling him that the 'Canons' made it up, but he doesn't believe me."

Then he will laugh, as his latest audience puzzles over what to make of this "broken down old drunk," as he describes himself. (Their puzzlement grows when the smiling ex-preacher retorts that Eddie "seems to be suffering from a rectal-cranial inversion" There are, of course, more common ways for people in the bar to say the same thing.)

Everyone laughs, especially Eddie, because he is my friend and knows he can trust me, two things we established long ago.

Ed says that while he has read the Old Testament two or three times, he has (as of the writing of this chapter) never read the New Testament—despite my frequent suggestions that he give it a try. He also tells people that he must be at least a little religious because he has his "own church" on his land, which is true. Sort of.

St. Olaf Lutheran Church, the first Lutheran congregation in our area, was started by a Lutheran circuit-riding pastor about 100 years ago. Eddie's ancestors donated the land for a church building.

Local Norwegian farmers and ranchers worshipped there whenever the itinerant pastor's travels brought him around, and eventually these parishioners started several other congregations in the region, including the first Lutheran church in Billings, Montana's largest city.

St. Olaf's still stands today, an old country church with a tall white steeple. It's the kind of lone prairie church you might have seen in an old western movie.

Though St. Olaf's has no resident pastor—and is no longer part of any Lutheran denomination—it still hosts the occasional worship service. Thus, Eddie can rightfully say that he "has his own church."

When I served the two-point Lutheran parish in Red Lodge and Joliet, Montana, I led monthly services at St. Olaf. Now, as Eddie's "favorite bar owner," I serve him beers as he and I talk about God in my bar. The irony is not lost on me.

Eddie is quick to tell Bull'n Bear patrons that he never went to hear the other "damn-fool preachers" who visited St. Olaf's over the years, but that he'd probably go to hear what I had to say if the roof didn't fall in because he was there.

Next story.

Our telephone rang at 7:23 one recent Saturday morning. I remember looking at the clock because it was *much* too early. Nancy and I had bartended the night before and didn't get home until about 2:30 a.m. Nancy handed me the phone, saying groggily, "It's somebody looking for Pastor Johnson." It had been 10 years since I had been *Pastor* Johnson.

"Hello, Pastor?" asked a shaky, unfamiliar voice, "This Al Herem."

Al was the husband of a former parishioner. His wife, Lynn, had been a wonderfully faithful member of the church in Red Lodge. One of their sons had served as a missionary pilot in Africa. Al, however, had little to do with the church, mine or any other.

During World War II, Al had served as a glider pilot. His unit flew in the Battle of the Bulge, but Al wasn't among them on that mission. At the end of a night training session, during the middle of a dust storm, his glider struck a tow plane that had crashed on the runway. Al was initially declared dead, but medics eventually brought him back to life.

That's why Al could not join his unit for the Battle of the Bulge, a unit that experienced 90-percent casualties before the last smoke had drifted away. Al knew that, if not for the training accident, he would have likely been among that 90 percent who had died for the sake of others' freedom, and he felt a little guilty that he was still alive when his friends had died.

Around Red Lodge, Al was known as a man with, shall we say, *eccentric* opinions, as well as a volatile temper. He sometimes drank excessively, at home rather than in bars, and this drinking had from time to time led to serious problems.

This was the man who was calling me way too early on a Saturday morning.

"Pastor Johnson," Al said, "I just had my fourth heart attack, and this one did some damage. I've decided it's time to get my things in order, and I wonder if you'd do me a favor.

"What's that," I asked, trying to disguise my exhaustion.

"Will you do my funeral?"

That woke me up.

"I could have the pastor at Lynn's church do it," he continued, "but he don't know my kind of life. You do. You know about people like me. I heard you do Ida Anderson's funeral, and I'd like you to do mine when it's time."

After we talked a little more, I suggested we get together at his house. "That way, you can get something that almost nobody else gets," I offered.

"What's that?" he asked.

"You can hear what's gonna be said at your own funeral."

"I'd like that a lot, if you don't mind."

We met at the Herem kitchen table. Lynn, always a kind and gracious woman, served coffee and cake.

I then told Al a few things he had no doubt heard from his wife and son. About Jesus, who forgives our sins. "We *all* need that." I said.

I talked about a loving and gracious God who deeply desires to have things made right between Him and all His children, including Al. And, of course, we discussed the promise of eternal life after we die.

When we were finished, he looked at me and responded with two simple words. "That's beautiful." He meant it, and I agreed. God loves beauty. That's why we are given something as beautiful as the gospel. That's why we share it.

Al, by the way, is very proud of his missionary pilot son. But he says that his son isn't really "like me" and doesn't understand "my kind of life."

For his funeral, Al wanted someone enough "like him" to talk about a "life like his." He believed he had found that person in me. A person with the right kind of credibility and authority.

Al's wife and son had told him about what God has done—and still is doing. He thought it was all *probably* true. But when someone who knew "his kind of life" told him the same thing, he was persuaded that this good news was not just true; it was beautiful because it was true *for him*. The gospel had gained an access point, something denied even to those who loved Al most.

Here's why I have told you about Eddie and Al. Each, in his own way, is like most bar people I encounter. They keep their distance from anything "church" because of a sometimes-unfair stereotype about Christians. What they are like and how they act.

More importantly, to Ed and Al, church people don't know about "their kind of life." Thus, church people don't have the authority to speak to them about Jesus—even though He *does* understand.

It's too bad, really, because, while some Christians really *do* come off as sheltered, there is a wide and varied (albeit *way* too quiet!) multitude of us who don't fit that stereotype at all. People for whom the peace and hope God gives has not shoved them into a boxed-in, church-approved lifestyle; rather, it has freed them to be who God made them to be, right where they are! They see a clear connection between who God has freed them to be and the work and social settings they live in. A logical connection between vocation and location, if you will. (And if they *don't* see clearly how their calling as God's children is linked to where they live and breathe, work and play, my experience is that they'd really *like to* see it!) They'd like to avoid the pressure, especially from other church people, to be someone other than who God made them to be.

Sometimes it's hard for us to grab hold of the fact that the secular business where we work or the bar where we socialize after work could be exactly where God wants us. (To some, the idea seems too good to be true; to others, it's intimidating). But God's mission happens where people live their everyday lives. It seems to me that God has put people in places—wonderfully varied and unexpected places—that allow them to share in His mission. On the farm or ranch. In a branch of the military. Or one of the places people go to relax or play after a hard day's work.

Some in the church, of course, don't think this way. Jesus had regular encounters with the Pharisees and heard their opinions about the sort of people with whom He should associate. (I believe that it was not only the claims that Jesus made about Himself that led to the crucifixion; it was also the sort of people He hung out with. Our Lord, however, didn't appear to be terribly concerned about appearing "acceptable." Sometimes He pushed back hard against such pressure. It could well be that, at least for some of those who listened to Him and believed in Him, Jesus' being among them and being *like* them was a source of His authority and credibility as an ambassador of God's Word. He knew "their kind of lives" and *still* loved them. Think of how much that matters, especially to people like Al!)

All of this has led me to conclude that if Jesus accepts us *as* we are—imperfections and all—His mission can use us *where* we are. That, in an effort to reach into the lives of *all*, the Holy Spirit uses even the "improper" Christians to bring the good news into the lives of fellow sinners: The good news that Jesus has come to reconcile us *all* to God. This leads me to a further conclusion:

Perhaps changing "those sorts" of people into "proper church people" isn't God's intention at all. Maybe He doesn't want us all to look and act alike. Shouldn't God be "allowed" the freedom to love us as we are and use us where we are—even though it's not always a neat, pretty picture?

Before we travel farther down this road, however, I need to clarify something: I am not proposing the religious version of "I'm Okay, You're Okay." Nor do I mean to take sin lightly. Sin is why we desperately need Jesus in the first place. Without Him, sin would spell doom for us all.

As I've said before, I am not introducing something new here. I am just talking about how God did in the past, and does still today use ordinary, work-a-day people to bring the sacred gospel to bear. Too often, Christians have placed unnecessary limits on how the gospel should be presented.

Let me elaborate. The reformer Martin Luther once wrote, *"It is perfectly clear in scripture that God accepts us just as we are; it is equally clear that God does not leave us as we are."*

Now, while I most certainly believe both parts of this statement, I wonder if we have twisted the meaning of its second half. After all, God's mission can take a wide variety of people into myriad situations as they try to fulfill it.

It seems that some Christians like to reverse the order of Luther's dictum. A person must become "acceptable" to God before God will accept him or her. (This is certainly the impression that the bar people hold. To them, Christians are like expectant parents who wait to see how a newborn turns out before accepting him or her as their child.) But that's not how God has chosen to do things.

A second problem is that Christians often want to dictate to God the specific changes that should occur when someone becomes a Christian. The Pharisees were masters at this, effectively removing the grace God had built into the Law.

I remember a story a pastor friend told of a woman who erupted in a "red-faced, veins sticking out" kind of anger over the story of Jesus' first "sign" or miracle in John 2. (When Jesus turned water into wine.) "Wine has alcohol, you know," she fumed. "How could He *do* that!" Maybe she'd find her answer in John 3, where Jesus says to Nicodemus, "The Spirit blows where it wills, and you do not know whence it comes or whither it goes." This may be one of the Bible's best statements on the breadth of things God can do and how God gets it done.

Simply put then, "God will not leave us as we are" does *not* mean He will change us all into something acceptable to other church people. It means He will change us into *whoever* He wants us to be. Servants equipped with both gifts and detriments, both of which God uses for accomplishing His mission in all kinds of places, with all kinds of people, everywhere in the world.

We are never "left as we are." But that doesn't mean all of our weaknesses and foibles will be magically removed. As Paul explains, the Holy Spirit can use even our weaknesses to help us spread the gospel. A weakness might be the thing that makes someone approachable and credible as he or she tries to reach out to a friend who needs God's grace and forgiveness.

As Al said to me, "You know about my kind of life...."

"I do," I replied that day. I had often wished that I *didn't* know so much about Al's kind of life. But I now consider it a wonderful, comfortable blessing of God.

If we are to cross the bar with the gospel—to be "one beggar telling another beggar where there is food"—it will probably not be done wearing starched shirts and holding a professionally written pamphlet.

More than likely, our best tool will be simply living an authentic life, being who we are. A life that will inevitably be full of foibles and sins, blessings and boils (for that is our nature), but also a life lived under God's overarching love and forgiveness. For there is power and authority in people who are at peace because they know, in spite of *who* they are, *whose* they are. Such people know whose mission they are called to serve, and they strive to serve Him with honesty and credibility.

What this looks like can take many forms. But here's what I've seen from my side of the bar, especially when those across from me are still trying to reconcile the whole preacher/bar owner thing: As I've noted, the Bible often has no authority for people like Eddie. And people with "proper lives" can't seem to get through to those who have lived life hard. (Even Al's own wife and son—whose brand of faith I honor and respect—couldn't seem to get through to him.)

For people like this, it takes a different kind of person to make a connection.

For me, this is part of the Incarnation's beauty. God came "in the flesh" to where people lived. The Incarnation proclaimed, via different methods, God's intentions to the wise (the Magi) and the simple (the shepherds). And then Jesus grew up and lived among regular people, like us, at ease and comfortable in His own skin.

To be sure, Jesus brought words of judgment, but we would do well to remember to whom these words were usually directed—the overly religious types who wanted everyone to live the same "boxed-in" kind of lives that they were living.

Which brings us back to Al Herem. For the sake of his country and the lives and freedom of those who lived in it, Al had been willing to climb into the cockpit of a glider and fly missions into enemy territory, directly over the heads of those who sought to kill him, understanding that he most likely would not return home alive.

These missions would be flown with no power but that of the wind, which both lifted him and held him at its mercy.

I'm pretty sure that Al was thinking that he was about to embark on a similarly dangerous mission the morning that he called me. That's why I wanted him to hear what I planned to say at his funeral.

For better or for worse, I am one who *does* know Al's kind of life. I'm ever so glad that, within God's mission, Al's life and mine could ride the winds together for a while. I'm also glad that God knows Al too, and loves him enough to proclaim to him (in words he can understand) the most beautiful message of all: That his last "flight" will be free of the fear of never returning. It will be a flight in which God's own mercy and the winds of the Holy Spirit will carry Al to where he is finally, safely home.

MARY-MARY

"Time can bring you down, time can bend your knees;
Time can break your heart, leave you begging please..."
From "Tears in Heaven" by Eric Clapton

THERE ARE TIMES IN OUR LIVES that seem to catch us so much by surprise that we become both startled and stunned when they occur, even though we know full well that it is a part of the very nature of those times that they will inevitably come—to every family, and to every single life. No exceptions.

Perhaps, then, it's not surprise that stuns us when death invades the family home as it is the overwhelming power that death wields when it finally happens close to us. Death has the power to turn our lives upside-down and inside-out. It affects everything. Our emotions, our thoughts, our actions, and even our perspective on reality itself. Our views on heaven, earth, and the meaning (or perceived meaninglessness) of life.

When death hits close to home, it's like being trapped in the churning waters beneath a waterfall. We are disoriented, at the mercy of the pounding waters and overpowering currents, fearing that we, too, might perish.

After this initial shock comes grieving—that terribly slow process of finally coming to the surface, gasping for the breath of life, and finally moving on, carried by life's currents, whether we like it or not.

Trying to make some sense of it all, as futile as that often seems, is part of grieving. So is moving beyond the need to fully understand why a death has occurred and simply embracing what God has done and promises yet to do. This is part and parcel of what Christians call the Gospel; the promise of life in the face of death. And it is in the God of the gospel of life, who stands firmly as Lord in the face of the law of death, that meaning for every life and every death is finally to be found.

Such has been the story of my friend Eddie.

Mary Weast, the daughter of Ed and Marilyn, was only 33 years old when she died.

She was engaged to be married to a very nice young man named Eric and was, in Bull'n Bear parlance, "full of piss and vinegar." In fact, sometimes we called her "Mary-Mary," because she was incredibly capable of being "quite contrary" when she wanted to be.

She was a strong, independent young western woman who loved life and lived like it. But she was no match for what hit her one March day.

About a week before Mary died, her doctors discovered a large non-malignant tumor surrounding her optic nerves and pituitary gland—and reaching all the way around to the back of her head and wrapping around her brain stem.

The tumor had shown signs of itself for several years, in part through terrible headaches, which were, at the time, diagnosed as migraines. Her doctors had prescribed pain medication strong enough to help Mary cope.

None of us thought any more of it in during those years. Meanwhile, the tumor silently grew. Even Mary didn't imagine that her headaches might be signaling something much more serious than a migraine.

But one morning she awoke with a terrible headache and blurred vision. Looking in the mirror, she saw that one of her eyes was pointing off in another direction, away from the mirror. Something was terribly wrong.

Only at this point did doctors discover the tumor, now large enough to put pressure on her optic nerves and physically cause one of her eyes to not track with the other. Mary was scheduled for surgery in two days. The surgeon would enter her skull through a nostril and excise as much of the tumor as possible.

When we learned about Mary's tumor and the surgery, the whole bar was stunned. Mary was a part of the Bull'n Bear community. She had bartended for a few years, was well-known to us, and well-loved.

Many people prayed for Mary, even those who, I imagine, did not spend a lot of time praying. Others requested that I say a "special" prayer for Mary, as I was the closest thing to a pastor that they knew. "You might have a little extra pull with the man upstairs," they would explain. It wasn't the time to argue the point, so I promised that my prayers would indeed join theirs, which of course, they did.

The day before the surgery, I called Eddie and offered to drive him the 70 miles to the hospital in Billings, so that he could see Mary beforehand.

Much to my surprise, Eddie said he wasn't going to go.

"I don't like hospitals," he explained. "I'll see little Mary when she gets home."

I had known Ed for a long time. He usually had a good reason for his decisions, even though he rarely talked about those reasons. I also knew, however, that he had a bad habit of missing important times in the lives of his immediate and extended family—sporting events, funerals, graduations, and the like. Why he had avoided such things, I do not know, but I do know that this pattern had caused some real, lingering hurt—especially with his kids and his ex-wife, as well as others.

Now I don't normally try to tell a man how to live his life, but this time I needed to make an exception.

"Ed," I said bluntly, "I'll be there tomorrow morning, and you're coming with me! This isn't about how much you hate hospitals. It's about a daughter who needs her daddy!"

Ed was silent for a moment as he thought it over. "All right," he said, as I knew he would. "I'll see you tomorrow."

The following morning, we drove to Billings to be with Mary.

At first, Ed seemed genuinely uncomfortable there in the hospital. But after we spent some time with Mary, and I said a brief prayer that God would watch over her and her surgeon, he seemed to relax a bit. He looked at me and said, "I'll be all right, Jim. Why don't you just go for a little while? I'd like to spend some time alone here with Mary."

When I returned about 45 minutes later, Mary's daddy told her that he'd be back to see her after she woke up from surgery. Then we drove back to Ed's ranch. During the drive, he thanked me for "making" him visit Mary. It may be one of the best things I've ever done for this leather-skinned, set-in-his-ways rancher who is my friend.

A couple days later, after Mary awoke from a drug-induced coma which served to keep her still while she recovered, Ed and I drove to see her again. Ed spent another wonderful hour alone with his "little Mary." As we left, he promised he'd return to see her again in a day or two. (Mary had survived a delicate first surgery, but another was needed.)

The next day, however, she fell victim to a raging infection that caused sudden and severe seizures, and her death. That wonderful hour the day before was the last hour Eddie Weast would share with his daughter.

Dealing with the aftermath of Mary's death required yet one more drive to the hospital in Billings. Driving home, Ed blurted out, "I hate those damned places! Everyone I've ever cared about who has gone to the hospital came out dead."

The cab of my pick-up grew silent. Finally, with a knot in my throat, I spoke to my broken-hearted friend. "Ed," I said, "I know that you and I have spent a lot of time bantering back and forth across the bar about God and all, but this is where the rubber meets the road. This is where God steps in and says, right in the middle of even death, that there's hope. That hope is what I believe Jesus is all about."

Ed looked at me from across the cab and said with a subdued anger words which I had never heard spoken out loud before, and which I shall never forget, for they seared into my being both the reason and the dire necessity for what God is up to in our world, and for my wanting to be a part of it among my friends.

"There *is* no hope," Ed said with deadly certainty. "Mary's dead, and I've got to get used to it."

By some grace, I had the presence of mind to avoid arguing the point (which I might have done as a young pastor). I don't remember what was said during the rest of the trip. Maybe nothing at all. Given the circumstances of the time, what could I say?

I returned Eddie to his ranch, the ranch where Mary was born and raised. As I drove back to the bar—where friends were gathered, waiting for news about Mary—I wept for my friend.

I soon discovered that the bad news had arrived before I did. I entered the bar to stunned silence. There would be no more laughing with Mary at the Bull'n Bear, as she drank a concoction of orange juice and Miller Lite. No more watching her, atop her horse, Buster, riding like a bat out of hell at the Home of Champions rodeo.

Mary wouldn't be joining Nancy for any more horseback rides.

Mary's funeral was held at St. Olaf Lutheran, the old pioneer church that sits on Eddie's land. She is buried in the cemetery adjacent to the church.

In the after-math, God got the blame for this tragedy from all quarters, though nobody said it out loud. It's odd, isn't it, how so many people in our culture have accepted as fact that God has nothing to do with our everyday lives—except when it comes to natural disasters (which even insurance companies call "acts of God"), or death.

You know what I mean, don't you, about God getting blamed?

"Why did God take her? She was so young," asked one of the grieving patrons sitting at the bar.

"I guess that God needed her more than we do," said another, trying to put some reason to it all. "She's in a better place now."

The father of an 11-year-old boy who had ridden horses with Mary explained it to him this way: "When the Lord wants you, He takes you, son. There's nothin' anybody can do about it."

As the days passed, I asked Ed how the battle was going. "I'm a little upset with God right now," he said, adopting an understated cowboy tone. "Why did he have to take Mary? Why didn't he take *me*? I've already lived my life." He took a long pause to swallow the sizeable lump in his throat. "I'm gonna miss that little girl," he said. A single tear welled up.

Now when a pastor addresses the faithful about the death of a loved one who shared their faith, he or she confidently proclaims a hope in which all can share. "Even in the midst of our sadness," he can tell mourners, "there is reason for joy."

And when preachers officiate the funeral of an unchurched person who they didn't know, they are insulated emotionally by their lack of familiarity with the deceased and his or her family and friends. Yes, there is the struggle to convey God's Word in a way that will reach the hearers, but a pastor in this situation stands before the gathered crowd often unsure of whether or not they will even attempt to listen.

But when you deeply desire to speak God's hope directly into the hearts and lives of your own dear friends—friends who rarely, if ever, think seriously about God—the task of speaking this hope "across the bar" becomes so heavy with emotional import that it's a burden almost impossible to carry, making the right words much harder to come by.

It was so sad to see all of Mary's friends and family struggling to face her death without knowing that there was anything else to do but cry, be angry, or drink? It was painful to see them slammed up hard against their great need of a savior—while not knowing if such a savior even exists.

They were in the middle of a storm, and they could find no hope of a safe harbor, much less the harbor itself. Well after the funeral, people continued to drift into the Bull'n Bear, saying things like "I just can't believe this!" and "Why did God have to take Mary?" I could almost see them suffocating from the lack of hope.

Mary's death and the responses to it showed me, more clearly than ever, why we who have been found by hope must faithfully proclaim that *hope* is what the church is all about! We simply must find ways to demolish the other stereotypes so that this truth will win out.

God's church bears the hope we have in Jesus. We must proclaim the unique peace and hope that are ours because of what God has done through the life, death, and resurrection of Jesus, for there is no one else to do it.

Many of those who grieved Mary's loss had seen the church only from a distance. To them, Jesus was someone who was watching them to see if they were living properly. They did not see the Jesus who gave His life for them in order to give life back to them. They had heard that Jesus "saves us from our sins" without understanding what that means: That is, by coming to live and die among us, and ultimately by rising from the dead, Jesus saves us—not so much from our sins—but from the death that sin brings with it.

Those without faith in Jesus tend to think the church is concerned mostly about their "bad behavior." But bad behavior isn't their real problem. The real problem is their terrible lack of any hope beyond what mere humans can provide for themselves. As a result of not knowing or understanding what God has done, they keep themselves so busy that they ignore their deepest needs. Or they numb themselves with alcohol or drugs, or distract themselves with television or the alternate reality of video games. (I can still see John and Sally, a couple about Mary's age, raising their glasses and drinking shot after shot "to Mary." Yes, they were attempting to honor her memory, but they were also trying to deal with their hopelessness, a hopelessness that was too big to handle sober. And these two weren't even close friends to Mary.)

It all makes me wonder: Why do so many of us whose deepest hope is Jesus content ourselves with showing the world a Jesus who is less than the savior we all desperately need? Why haven't we stood together and shouted "NO!" to those who preach a Jesus who is *not* the friend of sinners—instead of a Jesus who came to bring hope to us *all*? Why have we allowed "a different gospel" to supplant the true gospel?

For the gospel of Jesus is not, finally, about how we or anyone else behaves. Is it?

Nor is it about "correctness" of our beliefs.

It isn't about our "little sins," our "big sins," or how convincingly we repent when we sin.

The gospel of Jesus isn't about sin at all! It's about what our sin *bought us*, (sin's "wages" if you will): estrangement from God in our daily lives, and worst of all, estrangement from God in our inevitable deaths. The gospel is about what God alone can do. And He can do it all. In Christ, He has already done it. The gospel is about Hope, with a capital H.

If this is what we believe the gospel of Jesus Christ to be, what do we say about Mary to Eddie or Marilyn, to Eric, or to Mary's friends?

We say that God didn't do it, Mary's death. He *un*-did it. He took "that bastard death" and broke down its doors and provided a way through.

If we care at all about those who are without hope in God, *this* is what we should tell them. Not that their lives are wrong. *All* of our lives are wrong; deep down we all know that. Nevertheless, God has made us right because of Jesus, who died (just as surely as Mary died) to end death's reign. For death is God's *enemy*. As Paul said to the Corinthian believers, the risen Lord will eventually take full control on "the last day" of all that is. And on that day, "The last enemy to be destroyed is death."

This is why we needed a savior. Not to fix us up or make us more presentable, but to save Mary and Eddie and every one of us from the terrors and terrible loss of certain death. For Jesus' suffering and death were not the end of His story. And neither is our death, or the deaths of those we love, the end of ours.

This is what we say to those who love Mary. For this is where the gospel meets real life; where the ugly truth about death meets God's beautiful truth about life.

Ed Weast has told me many times that, even though he doesn't really accept the church's way of believing in God, "Any damn fool can see that there has to *be* a God. You can't watch a calf be born or a ewe lambing and not believe in God. Nobody but God could make that happen." He said this long before Mary died, back when it didn't matter so much to him.

A couple months after Mary died, when Ed was all out of hope and sure he'd never see his "little Mary" again, I drove out to his ranch to spend some time with him.

As we walked along Red Lodge Creek, which runs through his ranch, he showed me where a five-year-old Mary had thrown a hook baited with a worm into a fishing hole and "caught hold" of a rainbow trout that "went three or four pounds." Ed smiled as he told me how she had landed the fish. She simply threw her pole over her shoulder and ran toward the pasture until she finally dragged that beautiful rainbow up on the shore. (So much for us fly fishermen who "finesse" such a trout into our nets.)

On that walk, I told Ed how deeply I had been affected by what he had said as we drove back from the hospital the day Mary died. Then I asked him if he would be willing to think about something: "If God can create a life *once*, as you have said time and again that He does" I said, "what's to stop God from re-creating that same life once again? That's pretty much what Christians mean when we talk about the hope of resurrection and eternal life in heaven with God. God chooses to give us life again.

"I trust that, Ed. It is what gives me hope for my life, and hope when people I love die. That same hope is there for you."

"I'll have to think about that one," Ed finally said, breaking a long silence. Then we continued walking along the creek.

And he did think about it. I know this because a couple weeks later, while I was bartending, I overheard Ed telling a friend, "You know, I've been thinking . . . if God can create life a first time, why couldn't He create the same life a second time?"

Ed's still not sure about the answer to that question, but there's hope.

There is always hope.

When Wisdom Bends Her Knee

IT IS SAID THAT NATURE abhors a vacuum. What is true of physical nature seems to ring true of human nature as well.

In fact, when religion is discussed in a saloon like mine, you can almost hear that "whoosh" sound, like when you open a jar of canned peaches. It happens every time someone is about to hold forth on his or her understanding of God.

Now I don't know about other cultures, but in the Rocky Mountain West, comments from those not involved with the Christian church usually have something to do with the mountains, and with what's fair.

In this book, you'll hear a lot about the "My God is up in the mountains—that's where I feel closest to God and the most at peace" philosophy, and though it is a more distant God, there is, of course, evidence of God there. (It has become increasingly interesting to me that "peace" is often a part of such conversations.)

As for God and His fairness, some part of God's wisdom is to be found there as well. We've talked about this before.

I've heard many of my friends and customers say things like "I figure that if a person does more good than bad, God will have to take 'em into heaven. It all works out in the end."

These celestial scales of Good and Bad, which are present in most world religions, are almost always part of a discussion of barroom theology. (This theology, I should add, doesn't differ too much from that of some Christian churches.)

Almost never in these barroom discussions of fairness and creation, though, is God spoken of as being found through *revelation*—God revealing who He is.

Now, nearly everyone assumes that God, as a really good creator, must still have something to do with us, His creation. And nearly everyone believes that God cares about fairness and justice—about the balancing of those scales. But never have I heard a customer say that what they believe about their God was shown to them *by* God (as Christians believe it was in the person of Jesus). In some ways, this puzzles me, because a mere man or woman certainly wouldn't be able to "figure out a God" who could create such a vast and complex universe. It stands to reason that this kind of a God would have to reveal Himself to us in a way we could comprehend.

I suppose that one reason claims of God's revelation are never made is simply because it would be a conversation-stopper. People would think it was being disrespectful, a claiming of too much authority for their point of view. At the Bull'n Bear, it seems that no one wants to challenge his neighbor's opinion about God, even though I know that many there hold conflicting views of who God is and what He does.

In quieter, more private conversations however, things are different. Then the tones are hushed, people ask more desperate questions—and usually receive the grasping-at-straws kinds of answers that are the only ones available apart from God's revelation. These conversations grow even more frequent after a death—especially an unexpected death.

Such was the case with Cindy, one of our bartenders. After her husband, Bubba, died of a sudden heart attack, she struggled to find answers to her questions. She didn't find them in traditional western piety, for in the end, the "God of Creation" and the "God of Justice" is also finally a distant, inaccessible God. Nor did she find them in people like Sylvia Brown, who claim they can communicate with the dead.

These were the questions Cindy wanted to ask of God Himself but didn't know how.

God, of course, would welcome the questions, even if they weren't well-formed. God wants to be known by us, whatever our need or situation might be. That's what Jesus is all about.

There is, within all of us, a starting point. Most people believe that God exists—or at least they hope He does. God seems to have placed in each person a deep-down desire to know who He is, to discover what He's up to in the world in general and in individual lives. (Remember St. Augustine's statement: "Our hearts are restless until they find their rest in God.").

The biblical record is filled to the brim with examples that prove St. Augustine true. Consider the sailors who were unlucky enough to have the prophet Jonah in the belly of their boat. After they cried out, "each to their own gods" for help but found none, they turned to Jonah. They were horrified to learn that this man of God was running away from the One who had created both the earth and seas—the seas currently threatening their lives. Think about it: Would they have been so terrified if they doubted the existence of Jonah's God—or thought that their gods were just as powerful?

This brings us back to the gap between having an awareness that God exists and knowing Him in a deeply personal way. Absent revelation from God Himself, this gap cannot be bridged.

Case in point: Trevor, our poker dealer at the Bull'n Bear.

One Saturday night a few years ago, Trevor and I sat at the bar, waiting to see if anyone would show up for the game. While I'm not too clear how it came up—I rarely am—somehow the conversation turned toward our understanding of God.

Trevor's observation about this subject had to do with two fleas who lived on the back of a large dog and their struggle to discern the nature of this huge beast, who constituted their entire world.

According to Trevor's story, the two fleas held very different ideas on the dog's true nature. They would often sit back after a good meal and argue about the existence and essence of "dog." All the while, they lived on the dog's back, enjoying his warmth and his blood. Their lives totally depended on the dog.

To Trevor, this describes humanity, in relation to God. Like the fleas with the dog, most people have some sense that

God exists, but we can't understand who He is and what He's all about, or know Him personally—anymore than those fleas could have a meaningful personal relationship with the dog. "That's what I think religion is," to paraphrase what Trevor was saying. "Even though most of us agree that God exists, there's just no way we can know who or what God really is, much less really *know* God."

Here's the rub for we who are Christians: Trevor is right, at least partially. There *is* a vast difference between knowing that there is a God and knowing who that God is. And no one can truly understand and know God—unless God provides a way.

For most people, that vast and churning sea that exists between knowing there is a God, and knowing *who* God is, never gets crossed. Many don't even make the attempt. The journey seems too long and tedious—or just plain dangerous. In my observations from both within and beyond the saloon, fear is a major factor that keeps people from seeking God. It is far safer and more comfortable having God "over there," at a distance, where He can't meddle in our lives.

Thus, that gaping hole, signifying the need for God, gets filled with other things, whatever seems "copasetic," as a cowboy friend of mine likes to say (meaning "never mind if it's true, if it is somewhat satisfactory, that's enough.").

Even many Christians find it much more comfortable to keep God distant from their daily lives. Why? Because they know that God accepts us as we are but does not *leave* us as we are. And if I may use a sermon illustration I heard from Pastor Waldum," It is one thing to watch a circus performer push a wheelbarrow with his assistant riding in it across a high wire, 100 feet above the ground. You can see the feat and believe that the performer can accomplish it. It is quite another thing to get into the wheelbarrow."

My friend Eddie struck a similar chord after doing some reading in his first Bible. He observed that "It doesn't seem to pay to have Jesus come too near, if you happen to be one of those fig trees that aren't bearing any fruit."

So I understand why Christians keep God at a distance. They don't want to be like the fig-less fig tree and get in trouble for not doing what they were supposed to. It's harder to understand non-Christians' reason. I have spent years thinking and praying about this. These ponderings always seem to come to a head each time Christmas rolls around. I know that our annual "Christmas campfire," held at our home, will be surrounded by people for whom God remains far off in the distance.

To be sure, a few simply don't care about God or His proximity to them. At the campfire, they want to sing songs about Rudolph the Reindeer, not Jesus the Lord.

But for others, for those who *do* want to hear what I have to say when I speak to those gathered around the fire, I have come to wonder if, deep down, they fear that God simply doesn't care about them. Or to put it another way, I wonder if they fear that *God* might *want* that distance between Himself and us that they sense when they have only God's creation or justice to inform them.

What if, they fear, after finally turning to God for help they discover that He doesn't want to be there for them?

What if He doesn't want to help them in their time of desperate need. I think of Cindy: Her husband dies, and she finds herself wondering if Bubba's OK, wherever he is—and if she'll ever see him again. Is there anything she can do, like be "especially good," to make that happen?

After all, God's constant willingness to comfort His children in their time of need is not something you can see when your "church is in the mountains." Being in the mountains can be *peaceful*, but mountains can't give any real, lasting peace—especially in the face of tragedy—because they finally can't do anything about the tragedy that has happened.

Being in the mountains—or in the desert or on the sea or in the valleys or anywhere in God's marvelous creation—*does* teach us something true about Him, as does that innate sense of justice most people feel within themselves: "That which you sew, so shall you reap." Or, if I may put it in cowboy/trucker terms, "What goes around, comes around."

But in the end, our sense of justice falls short unless it leads us to Jesus who has shown us that God not only *is*, but is for us as well. We need rather to follow the lead of the Wise Men, who took the wisdom they had accumulated and nourished through the years—as imperfect as some of it was—and ended up kneeling before the young Jesus.

Jesus, God incarnate, bridges, once and for all, that vast distance between merely knowing God exists and truly *knowing God*. This is where we "get into the wheelbarrow," trusting the revelation of God, which we both desire and need. The incarnation, "God with us," is God's response to the restlessness, that vacuum in us all. It stands to reason, does it not, that if we are to know God as He wants to be known, He will need to show Himself to us? There is no mountain high enough, no understanding of the wisdom of justice deep enough, that can do this for us. God must do it. Our wisdom, like that of the Wise Men, must finally bend its knee in wonder and worship before what God has done.

Christmas by the Campfire

At Christmas time, I see a gleam in the eyes of many of my friends and patrons at the Bull'n Bear. For many of them, the fact that I'm a former pastor is especially ironic this time of year and I start hearing more religious jokes, shared, I presume, just to see my reaction. (Some of these jokes might seem disrespectful to us, but we have to remember that those outside of our fellowship don't share the same sensibilities as many of us.)

Here's one: The three wise men finally found the stable where Mary and Joseph were staying. The first two managed to enter the stable just fine, but the third was an exceptionally tall fellow, and he hit his head on the door jamb on the way in. In pain, he exclaimed, "Je-sus Christ!" Joseph looked at Mary and said thoughtfully, "How about that? That's a pretty catchy name!"

Another guy set me up one early December night by pretending to ask me a serious question:

"Say Jim, is it true that on the first Christmas, Mary had to ride on Joseph's donkey all the way to Bethlehem?"

I nodded, but I could see something coming.

"I know how Joseph felt," he said. "Last Christmas my wife rode *my* "ass" all the way to my in-laws' house in Wyoming."

❆　❆　❆　❆　❆

The first Sunday afternoon of each month, the Bull'n Bear hosts the "Old Friends Gathering," a dance for our older customers. "Norrine the Outlaw Queen" provides live music. (Norrine, now 80, claims she's been singing the "old country music" since it was new.)

After the December dance a few years ago, a man named Don and his dance partner, Vi, were making their way to the exit. Don stopped and told me that while they were Christmas shopping, someone had recently come up to him and said, "You know, whoever the guy was that started all this Christmas stuff ought to be strung up."

Don and I shared a moment of silence. The gleam in his eye told me that he, too, saw the irony of the comment.

The tradition of having a "Christmas campfire" with our friends from the bar started nearly 20 years ago. Nancy and I invite our friends from the bar—and anyone else who hears about it and wants to join us—to come to our home on Christmas night. We share with each other some wonderful clam chowder and other appetizers and a glass of wine or other libation. Then we wind our way through luminaries set in the snow next to the path that leads to the creek behind our house. There we stand around a campfire, sing Christmas carols, read one of the Christmas stories from the Bible, and I give a little meditation about why I think this night matters—for them and for the entire world.

While the Christmas campfire has become a wonderful tradition, however, the first one was neither cozy nor marked by warm fellowship.

On Nancy's and my first Christmas as a "blended family," we gathered our children (her two and my three) and headed down to Rock Creek. We built a campfire to observe the birth of Jesus, by ourselves. You see, even though several years had passed since "the affair," the divorces, and the remarriage, the sting of shame was still heavily upon us. We didn't feel comfortable showing up for the Christmas service at what had been "our church" in town. Nor, at the time, did we feel we would be welcome.

And so it was that, from difficult circumstances, a Christmas tradition was born. I brought my guitar, and we sang Christmas carols, drank hot chocolate, and stared at the fire. The kids placed long sticks in the fire, then removed them and held them high in the air, watching the smoke curl up toward the stars, like incense rising to heaven. I read the biblical Christmas story, as my dad had done when I was a child, and then Nancy and I talked with the kids about how God had come to be with us, small as we are, and why this matters.

We told Jim and Stena, newcomers to town and parents of a little boy named Maverick, about this and they joined us for our campfire the following year.

Subsequent years found others joining our group—others unlikely to attend church even at Christmas time. They sang carols, which they discovered had more than one verse, and they heard a Christmas story less familiar to them than the one about Santa Claus and his flying reindeer. They too stared into the fire, listening to and wondering over what God has done.

And so the tradition grew. Year after year people come by, often expecting one thing and getting quite another. Most of them are people we've met at the bar (although we met Cindy's husband, Bubba, for the first time down by the camp-fire). People arrive with their own ideas about God, but they depart with something more specific about what God is up to in this world God loves, about how God came to be one of us at Christmas time.

One year, I read the story of Mary, Jesus' earthly mother. Then we talked about what a wonder it was that God, creator and Lord of all, had even noticed Mary (who was, in our ways of viewing people, small and unimportant) and chosen her for such a sacred privilege. Just as it is a wonder that God thinks of us today, notwithstanding our smallness in the grand scheme of things. In front of the campfire that night, we thanked God for His regarding us.

At another campfire, we focused on the shepherds. Those gathered loved the shepherds—perhaps because shepherds seem more like bar people than church people. Nevertheless, God, who has regard for the lowly, thought so much of the shepherds that He sent angels to tell them a savior had been born to *them*! And the shepherds got the word before anyone else—even the religious people. Thankful hearts and silent praise rose with the smoke that night, around the same kind of fire those shepherds of long ago might have gathered.

The Christmas campfire I think I will remember the most, however, was not memorable because of a word that longed to be spoken. Instead, it was marked by something said by one who longed to hear.

This particular Christmas we had made a special effort to invite as many people to the campfire as we could think of, family, friends, and all bar employees and their significant others. Most said they would attend. Few actually did. The only ones who showed up were Jim and Stena with some of their family, one of our bartenders, and my mom, who was visiting us for Christmas.

Oh, and one more.

I never expected to see Eddie. He's never had much time for "such foolishness" as Christmas.

And he'd said to me, teasingly, a few times, "I've decided that alcohol and religion are a lot alike. Just the right amount can make you feel pretty good, but too much of either will get you into big trouble."

But this Christmas was the first since his daughter Mary died. Eddie showed up almost an hour early.

After he helped me build the fire, we went into the house and had some of the great clam chowder Nancy makes. We probably had a beer too. Then our small group went down to the campfire. I said a few words of welcome and explanation of how this all began, then led the singing of a few carols with my guitar. Next I read the Christmas story from one of the gospels.

I had scarcely begun my "Christmas meditation," when Ed interrupted. *"This is what I was hoping to hear,"* he said, staring into the fire. *"This is why I came."*

And as I continued with whatever I was saying, my heart—if a heart can do such a thing—turned up the corners of its mouth and smiled.

God had led us to this place. Some came filled with the wisdom of the world. Some came with deep wounds and an even deeper need for the hope only God can provide.

After we sang "Silent Night," I prayed for us all, that we, like the Wise Men, would bend our knees before the good things God has done, and that we would bring both our burdens and our hopes and lay them before Him, the God who has chosen to reveal who He is: The One who is *for* us by coming to be *with* us all.

An Unnecessary God

I RECENTLY HEARD A STORY about a fellow who wanted to build a bar on property close to a local church. Too close, in the church's eyes. In fact, the church didn't want another bar built anywhere. Bars, the church members claimed, had a negative moral impact on the community, especially on the children.

When the prospective bar owner publicly announced his plans, the church rallied around their pastor, who had railed against the "ungodly endeavor," everywhere from the pulpit to the town hall.

But the bar owner eventually broke ground, while the preacher broke into a sweat, and the church broke into prayer groups.

While the bar's walls were going up, the church circulated petitions, sought injunctions, and did anything else they could to stop the process.

The church carried out prayer vigils and fasts. They picketed. The pastor's anti-bar sermons became more fervent. But all the efforts were to no avail. The bar was completed, and a date was set for its grand opening.

The night before it was scheduled to open, the bar was struck by lightning. It burned to the ground.

The church held a public praise service and "gave glory to God." The service was so fervent that it seemed the whole community heard it. One week later, the church was slapped with a lawsuit. The suit alleged that the church had, "either directly or indirectly," caused the lightning to strike and the bar to burn.

The church denied any responsibility, and the case went to trial. After opening statements had been made, the judge studied the bar owner and the church representatives in attendance. "In all my years on the bench," he said, "this is the most unusual and surprising case I've ever tried. On one hand I have a bar owner who believes fervently in the power of prayer, and on the other, a whole church that doesn't!"

After 15 years in the saloon business, I'm rarely surprised by how bar people and church people look at God. But this past Easter was one of the exceptions.

Nancy and I invited our friends from the Bull'n Bear out to our home for a meal and a campfire down by Rock Creek. Our Christmas campfire had become a tradition, but this would be our first Easter campfire.

With guitar in hand, I led those gathered—believers and non-believers alike—in a few campfire songs. Then I read from the Bible and talked a little about the death and resurrection of Jesus our Lord, which, as usual, led to an "around the campfire" discussion about what Easter meant for us all.

I had hoped and prayed that there by Rock Creek, just as on that first Easter evening, eyes would be opened by

God's Spirit and that at least some of those gathered would see Jesus in a new light. That they would see what God has done and sense His presence.

After all, similarities to the setting of the biblical Easter-evening story and our own setting abounded: Friends sitting around a campfire, talking about the amazing events of a day that was unlike any other. Nearby there was water great for fishing. What more could I ask for?

As far as I can tell, though, the only eyes that were opened that Easter evening were my own. I didn't see anything as stunning as the risen Lord, but something did take me by surprise—and it hasn't left me alone ever since.

For all of our talk about Jesus' Resurrection that evening, I didn't sense that any in my audience (Christians or non-Christians) made any relevant connection between their lives and Jesus' being bodily raised from the dead. I felt the same disconnect about the promise of believers' future resurrection. It was as if no one had ever given a thought about being a person created by God as a physical body—that our bodies are inseparable from who we are. So why care whether or not that body would someday be resurrected?

After the fire tapered down and everyone had gone home, I sat alone by the flames and wondered about the glaring disconnect between the Easter story and the life stories of my Easter audience. After all, our *Christmas* evening campfires (featuring the story of Jesus' birth and the meaning of "God with us") were always received with eager, even joyful ears.

On this *Easter,* however, it seemed that most people couldn't leave quickly enough. Apparently, they somehow regarded their physical bodies as unnecessary when thinking about eternal life. Perhaps even bad. Thus, a resurrection of the body message had left them cold.

As I gazed into the fire and thought more about the evening, it suddenly dawned on me: These people had a different view of what it means to be a human being than the Bible presents. They had problems with the physical bodies God Himself created.

Now I was beginning to realize why the *same people* behaved so differently at Christmas and at Easter. At Christmas time, Jesus is seen as a baby "meek and mild," and we all love babies. Babies we can cuddle and hold. We can also put them in a crib or hand them to someone else until we choose to hold them again.

But Easter! To raise a body up from death requires both a power and will far beyond anything we can imagine, *much less control.* Easter *requires* that we take God seriously when He says, "I am the LORD your God!" For with this powerful statement comes the necessary corollary: "I am the LORD your God... *AND YOU ARE NOT!*"

In Easter we find a God who won't share the steering wheel with us. In Easter, God alone is God, doing what only He can do. That makes people, both churched and un-churched, uncomfortable.

But there is more to this "problem of Easter," something that affects *especially* the un-churched. During the campfire discussion, it became clear to me that for the non-Christians in attendance, the Resurrection story was essentially a spiritual metaphor for their belief in an "immortal soul," through which they will carry on a spiritual existence after their physical deaths. This belief is rooted in Greek philosophers like Plato, who separated the body from the soul, deeming the soul of greater goodness and importance. Thus, the "real person," the "good soul," needs to be freed from the corrupt and corruptible body.

In this view, the ultimate separation of soul from body is simply the nature of things. Not only *can* the body be freed from the soul, it *ought to be*. Further, this is not something we need God to achieve for us. It automatically happens when a person dies.

This philosophy is prevalent today, both outside and within the church. In the television show *The Ghost Whisperer,* for example, a young woman (with no aid from God) helps spirits who are "stuck" in the physical world after their bodies have died to enter "into the bright and beautiful light." The Ghost Whisperer frees these spirits by convincing them to "let go" of people and things they had loved here, on the physical, temporal earth.

Here's another example: Have you ever attended a funeral and heard someone say of the deceased, "I bet she's up there smiling down at us right now"?

Yes, it takes many forms, but the idea of a person's continued "spiritual existence" after death is readily accepted among most bar people. God isn't viewed as necessary in this existence. At most, He's the creator who long ago designed humans to have separable bodies and souls. After that, the process takes care of itself. It's just the way things are.

Surprisingly, many people who *do* believe in Jesus have almost exactly the same attitudes and beliefs. They give little thought to the "new creation" that God is bringing about now and will complete at the resurrection of the dead and the final establishment of His Kingdom.

As best as I could determine from listening to everyone at the Easter campfire, God's importance in the reality of life after death was negligible. Both Christians and non-Christians seemed confident that their souls would live on, quite apart from any new work of God. That was just the way things worked. Dying, then, was merely moving from one mode of existence to another. If God had any role at all, it was to determine if that movement was "up" or "down." Resurrection as a future work of God through Jesus didn't matter; whatever "immortality" these folks hoped to attain in the future, they already *innately* possessed.

I'm sure you can see why this belief system is such a huge obstacle for anyone hoping to cross the bar. Where immortality is innate, a given, there is no need for Jesus and what He accomplished for us in His death and resurrection. And you're left looking, as I was that night, at people who are like cows looking at a new gate. Something important is right in front of them, but they don't understand what it is.

My audience had missed seeing a wondrous God—whom they desperately need to be *their* God—doing something He alone can do. The God who *alone* has the last word on both their death *and* their life after they die. It is God who created their lives once (and apparently thought that making us as bodies was a good thing) and is essential for re-creating those lives again, after they die. They had, in effect, done an end run around the grave, or so they thought.

This viewpoint flies in the face of virtually all Christian creeds, which affirm the resurrection of the body—a resurrection through which God accomplishes what humanity desperately needs but cannot achieve on its own. For no one other than God can break death's grip. We can't do it for ourselves, Scripture says, and it certainly won't happen on its own.

If the Christian gospel of the resurrection of the body is reduced to something that is indistinguishable from the common belief in the innate immortality of the soul, then that which we have to proclaim about Jesus is robbed of it's power to give us life even out of real death. Then our belief in the resurrection of the dead itself becomes unnecessary. If Jesus gives us only what we have anyway (simply because we are human), why would we possibly need him?

But the truth is, God must act—the God who created us as we are, chose us, seeks and finds us. Furthermore, He saves us by doing something entirely new: re-creating life even out of death.

Those who do not know or trust in Christ, however, miss the vital connection between God and eternal life. By believing that they innately possess "immortal souls," their hope of eternal life exists quite apart from God or Jesus' death and resurrection. Many people around us operate under this misconception. They don't know the One who has done— and continues to do—it all. Thus, they are trying to cross a vast canyon with no bridge.

But if what Jesus has done *is* to have saved us even from death, which is what the church has proclaimed since it first began, then we have something new to say about everyone's desperate need for God alone to be God. This is the truth we need to proclaim, rather than trying to explain, for example, how one's body and soul finally "get it all together" in the end. For when we share this truth, who knows what mighty works God will do in the lives of those around us? What we do know for sure is that our words of hope will finally have the power to work in each person the new life he or she deeply longs for, but cannot possess apart from God.

Knowing the House
You Play In

WHEN A BAR HIRES A BAND, the band's job is basically twofold: 1) to make people get up and dance, and 2) when they're not dancing, to make them want to sit down with their friends, have a drink, and stay for a while.

Two kinds of bands typically play bars, regardless of their musical genre: those who read their audience and play what the people want to hear, and those who play only for themselves.

I quit hiring those who play for themselves. They don't get the job done. Most bar crowds just don't like a band that plays for itself.

*　*　*　*　*

It was one of those long, boring nights every bartender experiences when business is slow. There I was, with one of my locals. (I'll call him "Phil" because he's the kind of guy it's easy to get your "fill" of.) We were passing the time, with Phil carrying on about this thing or that, thinking himself to be one of the more clever people in the world.

He is also, unbeknownst to him, one of the first to encourage my hesitant steps along the path of crossing the bar. (Phil really encouraged me after I felt I had "bombed out" at a funeral I officiated—by boring people to death.)

At the time of this story, Phil was in his mid-60s. How he had lived so long without some guy decking him was a mystery to us all. As he readily admits, he likes to "devil people." Several times I have watched him aggravate complete strangers—sometimes big, strapping strangers.

I have been a victim myself. Shortly after Nancy and I began running the Bull'n Bear, Phil approached us, put his arm around Nancy's shoulder and gave her a good squeeze. "Isn't it nice," he said, "to have a real man take hold of you once in a while?" Then he laughed.

Another time when he pulled this same stunt, I thought the rancher who was his target would "pop him one," but he didn't. Phil said something to ease the situation. Laughter can defuse such situations, and laughter is one of Phil's great gifts.

It's hard to get mad at a guy who's just being himself. For decades, Phil has remained one of the most consistently politically incorrect people I know. But, somehow, he has been able to endear himself to most people he encounters. With Phil, even though you've never met him, you don't remain strangers for long.

Anyway, at about 9 o'clock on this slow weekday night, a woman entered the bar. The woman, whose name was Anne, had met Phil before (though he didn't recall it), but she was a stranger to me.

Anne looked to be in her mid to late 40s. She had a pleasant enough way about her as she ordered a double Grey Goose and cranberry juice cocktail.

As the night wore on, both Phil and I sensed something was troubling this woman.

Eventually, we learned that Anne had quit her job as a psychologist/counselor a couple years previously so she could take care of her ailing husband, the "love of her life." They had fought hard against his cancer, but it was a losing battle. Near the end, Anne's husband made her promise that, after a year had passed and she had had time to grieve, she would move on, both figuratively and literally, and embrace the next phase of her life.

This night happened to be the one-year anniversary of the death. Somehow, she felt that heading out to the Bull'n Bear was a way to start fulfilling her promise to her late husband.

(I saw Anne only one more time, again across the bar at the Bull'n Bear. This time, Anne confessed that her original plan that weekday evening had been to keep her promise to her husband, and then to return home and, by her own hand, "join him," because she was so terribly lonely. I do not know what changed her mind.)

Phil and I, of course, knew nothing of these plans, and even though Phil was "just being Phil," it didn't seem to daunt Anne. All in all, it seemed to be quite a pleasant night. The mood was light enough—and we laughed enough and had enough drinks together to put at least a few bucks into the night shift's till.

Somewhere during the midst of our conversation (Anne, Phil and I were the only ones in the bar for most of the night), Anne turned to us and, quite out of the blue, asked this question:

"How do you want to be remembered by your children after you die?"

Phil's answer was typically "Phil-ish,"

"Oh, I don't think my kids will remember me at all," he said. "In fact, my kids will probably try to forget me as soon as they can." Then he laughed, even though it wasn't all that funny.

Then Anne turned to me.

"How about you?" she asked.

Uncharacteristically astute, Phil somehow knew that "deviling" wasn't really in order and kept quiet. As I answered, I found myself expressing things I had never really thought of before.

"I think I would like to be remembered by my kids exactly the way that I will remember my own dad," I said, "and I'm not saying that just because I love him—he is my dad, after all—but I can't think of any man I've ever met that I respect more than I respect him and how he has lived his life."

Anne thought for a moment. Phil continued with his atypical silence, and the conversation soon turned to other things—things less serious. Before long, it was closing time and we said our "good nights."

I didn't think about that night again until years later, when I told this story to my best friend on our way to fish in

Yellowstone Park. "Do you have any idea," my friend said, in a dead-serious voice, "how few people can say that about their own dads?" Until then, I hadn't.

My parents gave me and my siblings a wonderful gift. They lived lives that consistently earned our love and respect. We listened to what they had to say, even when we didn't like it.

So how does the way I want to be remembered by my kids, and how I continue to regard my parents, relate to crossing the bar?

If you live an authentic life, that is, if you "are who you are," you can be secure in who God created you to be. Further, people will trust you, and the importance of being trustworthy simply cannot be overestimated. For if any of us want to be listened to when we talk with others about important things (such as how much God values us and what He's done to prove it), we must first build a firm foundation of trust and friendship. That foundation cannot be built without authenticity.

To "live a life that is worthy of your calling," as the apostle Paul put it, is not so much about being morally pure or politically correct. As I've lived and worked in the bar, I've seen that bar people don't put heavy emphasis on living according to the letter of the law. Bar people have different values, and if we Christians want to connect with them, we had better learn that lesson well. Like a good band, we need to "know the house" we're playing in.

To "live a life that is worthy of your calling" among the bar people means avoiding the trap of having your actions speak so loudly that people can't hear what you're saying. With bar people, for example, coming off as overly pious conveys the messages: "I'm better than you are," and "You're not good enough."

Bar people respond to those they understand and trust. They want mutual respect. So "giving an account of the hope that is within you" might be best achieved as one beggar showing another where to find bread.

Sharing the gospel is not a random sales pitch. We must be discerning about what we share, and with whom. Time and again, I have heard that the most important factor in someone's really hearing the gospel was that the Good News came from a trusted and respected friend.

I cannot overstate the importance of building that relationship of trust and respect. Without it, we can't even begin to speak God's word of hope into people's hearts—especially at life's hard times.

Chief among these hard times is death, and one's desire to someday be reunited with a departed friend or family member. Bar people care as deeply about things like this as the rest of us do, much more than they might ever vocalize.

Or to say it another way, they care deeply about the hope we Christians have in Christ Jesus, the Lord of life. They just don't know it. They could know it, though, if their believer friends—who have built a foundation of trust and respect in their day to day relationships with them—show up to share the good news when the right time comes. This is the essence of crossing the bar.

Christians don't need to avoid the bar (or leave it). Just the opposite: The bar (whether literal or figurative) can be the exact place those who carry the hope should be. They "know the house." They know how to play the music their friends (bar people) can dance to.

The apostle Paul once said, "To those outside the law I became as one outside the law—not being without law toward God but under the law of Christ—that I might win those outside the law. To the weak I became weak so that I might win the weak. I have become all things to all men, that I might by all means save some." (I Corinthians 9:19-24)

Paul wasn't like a musician who played only for himself. He wouldn't demand that the "bar people" leave where they were and come to him to meet Jesus. He took the incarnation of Christ seriously. He left his home and went out into the world and brought Jesus to the people.

This is the example we should follow. For if the Incarnation teaches us anything about the mission of God in this world, it's "Play to the house you find yourself in, never just for yourself."

A Hard Case

—OR—

HOW TO GET FROM THE CHURCH TO THE BAR

We used to have a "time clock" of sorts at the Bull'n Bear.
Customers could "clock in" and win prizes. Prize or not,
each customer would walk away, with a small slip of paper,
bearing a proverb similar to the fortune in a cookie.
One day I punched in just for the fun of it. I received a
Russian proverb: "The church is near, but the road is icy.
The bar is far away, but I will walk carefully."

ONE EARLY WINTER'S EVENING, near the beginning of Nancy's and my career as bar owners, I overheard a conversation between my wife and Kathy, a 50-something elementary school teacher near the Crow Reservation about 80 miles from Red Lodge. As they sat at the bar talking, Kathy began explaining how she had made the journey from the church to the bar.

"I was a member of the Presbyterian church in my home town," Kathy said. "I was pretty active, too. I used to teach Sunday school and everything... and then I got divorced.

"When the word got around that I was divorcing my husband, no one at church talked to me for three weeks in a row. I left, and I haven't been back since."

What a shame, I thought to myself.

Kathy's story took me back to the days a year or so after I had left my parish ministry. I was doing a brief concert tour of Lutheran churches in northern Oregon.

During the concerts, I performed a song I had written about divorce. The song lays bare how divorce feels to the couple involved, and how the reactions of people in the church can make the pain even deeper. It also speaks very bluntly about God's grace.

The song is titled "A Hard Case," because that's what a divorced person often experiences God to be. The same can be said of the church. Both are frequently perceived to be "hard cases." Of all the songs I've written or sung, this one gets the most response.

On that Oregon tour, three women in three different towns approached me after the concert. Each told me she had been deeply affected by "A Hard Case." Not surprisingly, each had a story similar to Kathy's. While their marriages and their whole lives fell to pieces, they became isolated from their churches. They felt they had failed themselves, their churches, and even God Himself.

Unlike Kathy, each of the women, in her own time, had returned to the church. But it was a slow process. It took one woman 10 years, another 18. The woman who had been the most involved with her congregation (she was the church secretary) also suffered the longest absence. It took 30 years before she came back. Thirty years without hearing God's Word, receiving the Sacraments, or benefiting from the accountability, love, and acceptance of her church family.

Eventually, several years after Nancy and Kathy's first conversation, Kathy accepted one of Nancy's invitations to "join us by the river" for one of our Easter campfire services. After that, she slowly became a regular part of our little "crossing the bar" community of faith. There she's listened to God's Word, shared the Sacraments, and participated in our small band of freedom, love, acceptance—and reconciliation.

None of these women's long church absences should surprise us. Early in my pastoral career, I heard this statement: "The church is the only army that shoots its own wounded." Sadly, this adage is true.

A poll taken by the Methodist church found that approximately 80 to 85 percent of church people who get divorced eventually leave their congregation, never to return. One has to assume that few of these people are asked "Please stay." Perhaps fewer still are sought out and asked "Please come back."

What a shame! Or perhaps I should say, "What shame!" All too frequently, shame is the center line on the road that leads hurting people farther and farther away from the church. And unless someone stands in the middle of the road with open, embracing arms, it's a road of no return.

Where do these hurting, broken people go? Most often, they run into whatever arms are open to welcome them.

Sometimes, of course, this means "going from the frying pan into the fire." They try, too quickly, to replace one romantic relationship with another. This rarely works out well.

Before the paperwork is signed and a divorce is final, one or both members of a divorcing couple often become involved in a new romance. I've seen estimates as high as 70 to 80 percent. However, in my experience, infidelity is not the No. 1 problem in most broken marriages. The "other man" or "other woman" is simply a way to seek comfort or relief during a really painful time.

All sorts of other things cause a couple to cease living out what God intended their marriage to be; a new romance is often just the "match" that ignites the years of accumulated trash, finally burning the house down.

But regardless of the specific circumstances, whenever a church member's divorce involves *any* kind of extramarital romance, the shame for them is almost unbearable. (Especially given the fact that most churches regard anything sexual as especially immoral, even "dirty.") The divorced person believes he or she is a failure—a failure at one of the most important endeavors in life: maintaining a healthy family. This can lead to feelings like, *I'm not the person I've always thought I was. I thought I was a better person than this,* feelings that are piled on top of the feelings of *I'm really not the person "they"*(the church) *think I am.*

It shouldn't be so strange, given the turmoil of a failed marriage, to see men and women clinging to someone who accepts them just as they are. In the darkness, they feel accepted and loved, while in the light of day, they see nothing but a cliché, a label, a failure; someone who is seen by others as unfaithful, immoral, and just plain dirty. If they think this is how their own church community sees them, it's not so hard to understand why they don't want to be there.

There are a multitude of failures in any divorce, and any divorced person knows this, but perhaps we as the church need to shoulder some of the blame as well. Remember Jesus' words to the "immoral" woman in John 8: ". . . neither do I condemn you; go and sin no more."

Sex and the Church

When a couple divorces, blame and shame are not what they need from their church. This is a case in which the Body of Christ needs to reach out with embracing arms and practice what it preaches.

At this point in our discussion, we can't continue to explore the church's response to divorce without touching on the church's attitude toward human sexuality.

For some people, of course, sex is just sex. I have certainly seen more than my share of people who feel that way. (One of the things that Nancy and I have been most proud of about the Bull'n Bear is that we've earned the reputation as a "safe place" women can go, with no fear of being hassled by some guy whose testosterone level is off the charts. We insist that everyone is treated with respect—including the bartenders.)

But the "sex is just sex" attitude is the exception, not the rule, especially for those going through the breakup of a marriage.

This brings us back to the church. Because the church seems to be so unwilling to talk openly and honestly about sex in any way other than one that begins with the words "Thou shalt not...," it has failed to understand (much less proclaim) that our sexuality is an integral part of who God created us to be. Or to put it bluntly: The church has failed to accept the simple fact that sex, which plays a huge part in who we are as men and women, plays this role *by God's own design*!

When sex between two people is in concert with what God intended it to be, it imparts an acceptance of one another. It is part of a relationship that is not only trusting but helps to further build trust, creating in that home a *trustworthy* world. It's the opposite of shame.

This is why misusing sex, giving something of ourselves via a relationship without that foundation of trust and commitment, often leaves a person feeling empty and alone. Feeling *worth less* than he or she was created to be and less able to trust another.

There is a deep and abiding grace built into God's gift of sexuality—something close to the core of what it means to be created "in the image of God." When a man and woman join together according to God's plan, their intimacy mirrors the interrelationship of the Father, Son, and Holy Spirit. It's an intimate, trusting, and trustworthy connection shared by two people who love each other and are deeply committed to one another.

It is no wonder, then, that God protects physical intimacy with the commandment which says, *"Don't misuse this gift!"* It is too precious to ever be treated without regard for God's purpose.

We in the church should be able to talk openly and matter-of-factly about sexuality. Otherwise, those outside the church have little hope of understanding this wonderful and powerful thing as a gift from God. For they are not hearing from us the message, "Don't misuse God's wonderful gift of sex." They're hearing, "Don't use this gift at all. And if you simply must use it, at least don't enjoy it! It's dirty." Sadly, the church occasionally gives the impression that this message applies even to married couples.

Case in point: One Sunday morning, a pastor friend of mine announced from the pulpit that he and his wife had adopted a child. After the service, a woman from his congregation approached him and shook his hand. "What a nice way," she told him, "for a pastor to have a child!"

While it may be true that the greater the gift, the greater the potential for misuse, the church seems to have focused almost exclusively on the *misuse* of the gift. We've forgotten to give the gift its due.

Christian traditions like mine have focused almost exclusively on the (very real) need for the *redemption* of God's creation, which happens through Jesus. But we've done this to the exclusion of remembering God's gracious intention in creating this world, including sexuality, in the first place— and His sending the Holy Spirit to continue the creating and redeeming work in the world every single day.

This misplaced emphasis results in our neglect to tell the world that the same loving intention we see in all Jesus has done was *first present* when God created the world. When "God spoke…and it was so…and behold, God saw that it was good."

It's no wonder that many bar people find the church irrelevant. No wonder so many of them say, "My church is in the mountains," for there such attitudes against the created order don't apply.

The Open Arms of the Bar

Sometimes, the open arms divorced church people run to hold no promise of romance. Sometimes church people seek friendly refuge in the bar people, those of us who seem to accept them just as they are. In the bar, these hurting men and women find a place where they don't feel that sense of shame so sharply. They feel like they are among equals.

This is no accident. Most of us sitting on barstools are well aware that we have, at some time or other, pretty much screwed up things in our lives. So who are we to judge? And when someone gives voice to the obvious, expressing "deep bar wisdom" like "Sometimes you're the windshield; sometimes you're the bug!" the ice between the "regulars" and a newcomer starts to melt. And the shameful big red "A" that someone feels hanging around his neck can be hung up at the door of the bar.

It's all so sadly ironic.

Among places that the church discourages people from frequenting, the bar is often No. 1. For many, however, the bar is the one place that a shame-filled church person can find the embrace of acceptance. For Kathy and many others, the bar is the community of the Broken Yet Still Accepted, the kind of community that the church has long proclaimed itself to be.

The Misuse of Shame

A big part of the problem is that the church seems often to have viewed shame as a tool for controlling people's behavior. Rather than viewing shame as an ominous symptom of something gone terribly wrong in God's wondrous creation, the church has appropriated and used it like a weapon on people, from the cradle to the grave. (This is not true of the church all the time, of course, and I don't mean to imply anything even close to that, but it has been and remains to be true often enough.)

Consider, for example, some churches' refusal to serve Communion to the divorced, or to the divorced-and-remarried. These people already suffer from a deep sense of shame, and now they are being told, "You're not welcome to receive the forgiveness and blessings Communion represents. You're a sinner, you know." No one vocalizes these words, but the message is not lost on those who live in shame. And the shame overshadows even the gift of God that is present in the elements and practice of Communion, where God is the host.

The church correctly understands that divorce is outside of God's intention; it is sin, another example of "missing the mark" of what God first intended for us. But must we not immediately ask "what is the gospel's response to sin?" In this case, the church often fails miserably at applying the answer to that question: forgiveness, the forgiveness that reaches deep into the core of our being and reconciles us to God and to God's people.

After all, even the biblical prohibition against divorce is rooted in love and grace. Given all of the pain and shame that accompany divorce, it is no wonder that God would try to keep us from them, just as any loving parent tries to protect a child from harm.

Martin Luther once said that, because we are sinful creatures bound to seek what *we* want rather than what God intends, we will get ourselves into problems with no good solutions. In other words, no options, save those that are outside of God's original, loving intention for us.

Divorce is a prime example. To remain in a relationship that is harmful and miserable for both people is not God's intention for marriage. And of course, the divorce that ends such a marriage is outside of His intention as well. In these situations, Luther said, all that is left to us is to choose the lesser of the evils, "sin boldly" and trust in the grace of God to forgive even this, allowing us to leave it behind and once again seek to live within God's loving intention and to participate in His mission.

Unfortunately, the grace that allows for a new day to come, for life to arise even from this kind of "death," is often missing when it comes to the divorced sinner and the church.

I speak from experience. One of the hardest lessons I learned early in my own journey is that my church, which was exceptional at proclaiming God's forgiveness, was equally exceptional at making sure that my shame before God's people *remained*. ("Of course God forgives you," I was told, "but this isn't a matter for forgiveness.").

Even in its proclaiming God's forgiveness and mercy, the church has frequently failed to be a true and faithful ambassador of reconciliation between both God and the body of Christ. When the church fails at this task, the painful reality of shame remains even after God forgives a person and restores His relationship with him or her.

Such shame is terribly powerful. Shame pays no mind to who bears which percentage of blame in a broken relationship. Its mission is to control and destroy what God has created.

And destroy it does! Shame robbed me of so much.

The first thing lost to me (besides my positive sense of self) was the church I loved. Even though I moved far from the scene of my broken relationship, every time I entered a Lutheran church I felt like I was "glowing" with shame. I hated being asked questions about myself, such as "Where are you from?" and "What do you do for a living?"

When I finally moved back to Red Lodge, the town where all the trouble occurred, it took me more than 10 years to darken the door of either of the two churches I had served in. (This is why our "church by the river" began. Nancy, our children, and I didn't have anywhere else to go to worship God.)

The long-time absence of a church in my life resulted in another casualty: My understanding of God and His loving involvement in our lives.

My sense of shame created a distorted view of myself. As I considered the vastness of creation, I felt unworthy of God's attention. (What finally brought me around? Even though our smallness in the scheme of all creation is undebatable, I could not call Jesus a liar. *He* said that God cared, and I clung to that for dear life.)

I didn't even really notice yet another effect of shame until someone pointed it out to me. Since my teens, I had expressed my thoughts and emotions through songwriting.

Shame led to an almost-15-year dry spell. I defended myself by saying that my "muse" had left me. In truth, it was my sense of the "self" that God wanted me to be that was missing.

I returned to songwriting only at the coercion of a friend, who wanted me to write a song for a conference he was scheduled to lead. He helped me finally be reconciled to myself.

Now I suppose I've been pretty hard on the church, but I maintain that the church's use of shame in people's lives makes the criticism valid. God calls to us to seek healing for the person suffering from shame.

To preach a forgiveness that doesn't include the shedding of shame is to preach a gospel that doesn't touch the core of our beings. Such a gospel is no gospel at all. It's a bandage placed over a festering wound, leaving a wound that won't heal.

Further, because the church affects people's perception of God, it's vital that we help the hurting take their shame and lay it at the foot of the cross. There, it will be more than merely forgotten. It will be destroyed, so that it cannot destroy the one who once bore it.

I need to say one final thing about the power of shame and those who leave the church because of it. Shame's *power* in one's life finally doesn't come from church or any other outside source. It comes from within.

We've spent many pages exploring how the church sometimes uses shame as a tool for control, but we need to understand that this "external shame" would have no power if not for the enduring sense of shame that we carry around inside us. Like it or not, we still find ourselves back in the Garden of Eden, hiding in the bushes from God.

The Shame Within

Hanging on one of my walls is the Talmudic saying I shared with you back in the Introduction: "We do not see things as *they* are; we see things as *we* are."

The wisdom of this statement is evident in divorce. In relation to the church, the shame divorced people feel does not come primarily from judgment or disapproval the church wields. It comes from the guilt and shame that already exists within us. Our sense of failure at one of life's essential elements: family. This sense of failure is all-encompassing. It churns inside of us and washes over us. There is no failure that is felt more profoundly than the failure to maintain a family.

I don't know exactly what Kathy faced with her church, but it is possible that some of her fellow church members wanted to talk with her but simply didn't know what to say. It's also possible that their silence came from a more liberal bent, which views silence as a way of expressing tolerance for others, even though it is not perceived that way by the one experiencing the silence.

The problem with both types of silence, of course, is that the interpreting of it is left up to a person who, based on all he or she is feeling inside, will most likely chalk it up to judgment.

The community of the Cross stands together on level ground. We all need forgiveness for missing the mark of who

God intended us to be, and in a myriad of ways. We're all at risk for sinking into the mire of shame, but the gospel says we don't need to sink. For "if anyone is in Christ, they are a new creation; the old has passed away. See! The new has come. And all this is from Christ, who has reconciled us to himself...and *has given to us* the ministry of reconciliation." (2 Corinthians 5:17-19).

This is the way back, not only for those facing shame, but for the church as well. It is the way back to God and to a more healthy and godly view of ourselves and our community of faith—godly not in the sense of what we do and don't do, but of who we *are*.

When our little community of faith meets every other Sunday down by the water, we often pray that we will *seek to be nothing less, but also nothing more, than what God intended us to be.* This prayer is for us as individuals *and* as a community of faith.

To seek anything else would truly be a shame.

Home by Another Way

I'D LIKE TO INTRODUCE YOU TO JACK, a far different Jack than we encountered in Chapter 4. This Jack is a cowboy who has lived most of his life, both at work and at play, out-of-doors. He's worked a ranch and served as "camp cook" on guided tours in the mountains he loves. On his days off, you can find him hunting or fishing.

Now in his 60s, Jack tends bar in a neighboring town. When he visits the Bull'n Bear, he likes to remind me that "people sell to people." What he means by this is that people don't visit a bar primarily for a drink; most of them come in to socialize with other patrons—and the bartender.

Jack doesn't have much good to say about organized religion, so he also loves to tell me preacher stories, hoping to "devil me" a bit. Sometimes these stories tell me more about Jack than about the preacher in question.

"Seems this old cowboy was riding back to the ranch house one day," Jack began a recent tale, "when he came upon a bunch of church people in the woods, lined up by the river to get baptized by some preacher. The cowboy didn't know much about this custom, but he was getting old and thought to himself that this gettin' baptized might not be such a dumb thing for him to do. Just in case. So he gets off his horse and gets in line.

"After being dunked by the preacher, he is pulled up from the water, only to hear the preacher ask, 'Did you see Jesus, brother?'

"The old hand responds honestly, saying 'Well, no, I didn't.'

"So the preacher dunks him in a second time, this time holding him under for a little while longer.

"'Did you see Jesus *this* time, brother?'

"'Well, no—

"But before the cowboy can finish his sentence, he is shoved back under for a third time, and held under even longer. When he is pulled back up, sputtering and coughing, the preacher asks loudly one last time:

'Did you see Jesus *this time,* brother?!' The cowboy, shaking the water off of his head and out of his ears responds in near panic, *'Are you sure this is where he fell in?'*"

Beyond being a pretty good joke, this story reveals a truth about the people with whom I work and play. Maybe that was Jack's point. None of them want to get into a situation that could make them look like a fool. And they're sure that's what would happen if they went to church, because they don't know even the most basic thing about a worship service or church doctrine.

They fear being shamed—not the kind of shame portrayed in Chapter 10, but shame nonetheless. A fear of being embarrassed or being made to feel like "you don't belong here."

In his book *Welcoming the Stranger*, my friend Pat Keifert points out that many people want to learn about God and worship with their neighbors, but the fear of not fitting in keeps them away. They don't know how to "do church," and they assume that everyone else does. They fear that they will be "found out" in public. They imagine they will be like the cowboy who shows up at a banquet—wearing old blue jeans, a sweat-stained hat, and cowboy boots—while everyone else is decked out in tuxedos and formal gowns.

Let's imagine the cowboy from Jack's joke, wandering into a mainline church service on Sunday morning. First, he encounters the "official greeter," who loudly welcomes him as "a *stranger* to these parts."

Then our cowboy is invited to sit down in a long wooden chair named after something that describes how his boots smell (pew). The kindly blue-haired lady next to him hands him a book as the liturgy begins. A strange formal conversation begins between the preacher and his congregation. The words and phrases sound like they are from a foreign language.

After this strange dialogue has gone on for a while, the service segues into a reading of Bible stories. Everyone else seems familiar with these stories and their lead characters, but the cowboy is befuddled. Are these stories actual historical accounts? Parables? Moral fables?

Next, the preacher gives a speech, apparently based on the recently read texts. The centerpiece of the speech is Jesus, a name the cowboy has both heard and spoken often, but never in this context. Apparently, this Jesus was once dead, but now He's not. Everyone in the congregation seems pretty glad about that.

A loud, unison "Amen!" startles the cowboy. Following this, the preacher invites the congregation to "pass the peace" (whatever that means). Then a plate containing little white envelopes is passed among the congregation. *What's hiding in those things?* he wonders.

The service continues with a short story about a supper at which Jesus was betrayed. After the story, everyone is invited to line up before a table. The cowboy lines up, because that's what everyone else is doing. A small wafer is given to each person. It looks like a miniature flattened piece of bread, but the preacher calls it "the body of Jesus." The congregation also receives tiny shot glasses of wine, which is referred to as "Jesus' blood," blood which "proclaims the death of Jesus until He comes again."

Finally, some songs are sung. Everyone but the cowboy seems to know them.

You get the picture, right? If you don't, imagine yourself walking into a neighborhood bar wearing your "Sunday best." People are talking and laughing, but they stop, turn around, and study you. Immediately, you feel that you don't fit in. You order a ginger ale and sit at the end of the bar, outside the conversation. You hear words you certainly don't encounter at church or around your house.

Church people often say of the unchurched, "They know where the church is; if they want to come, nothing's stopping them." But it's not that simple.

Mixed Messages

If the church is anything, it's a body of people who understand their dire need for the God who created them. They are grateful that God, through His son Jesus, has come to them, to reconcile them to Himself and to one another. They also know that God wants them to share this good news with others whom God also loves. This is what the church has been all about since the beginning.

Unfortunately, almost from the beginning, some people in the church have looked down on "those kind of people." Thus, they created religious rules that have proven to be barriers to God's mission of reaching the world with His love. The Bible is filled with examples.

Jesus was often criticized for being the "friend of sinners." He was criticized for allowing "that sort of woman" to touch Him by washing His feet with her tears (Luke 7:36-50). He was chastised for eating with, drinking with, and accepting those outside his own religious community and tradition—without preconditions. (See, for example, Luke 15: 1-2.) He even partied with "those kind of people" (John 2). For Jesus, this criticism and chastisement reached their peak on the cross.

Later, as the Christian church was beginning to grow, Peter—even though he had spent all that time close to Jesus—needed to be shown (in a vision from God) that the barriers that blocked outsiders needed to come down. In other words, the church "must not call 'unclean' that which God has made clean" (Acts 10).

Similarly, the apostle Paul, who was once convinced that his religious duty was to persecute, prosecute, and even put to death the *Christian* outsiders, was redirected by God from his cruel mission by being knocked off his ass (literally), blinded, and then given a vision and new mission (this time in concert with God's).

Paul was led to some of the same people he had once sought to kill so that he might be healed by them (Acts 9). Then he was sent out into the desert, where the risen Jesus instructed him to invite into God's Kingdom the very people he once thought didn't belong there (Galatians 1:11-24). Paul was told to shake off his religious tradition and go into "the world" that God "so loved." He found himself serving God in ways and places he had never imagined. To my knowledge, no one other than Jesus has ever wielded such a far- reaching influence in spreading the gospel (and the freedom it affords) as Paul.

We find ourselves in good company, then, when we go "home by another way" as we fulfill God's mission. When we go out into the world, as Jesus did, rather than demanding that the world come to us.

"My church is in the mountains."

I can't count how many times I've heard this excuse from people who want nothing to do with the organized church. After a while, I came up with a standard response:

"Boy, I hear you there. There are lots of places to see evidence of God in His creation, and even wonderful places to worship.

"*But*," I would add quickly, "the mountains can tell you only so much about God. They can tell you that God is a pretty good creator, but when things get all messed up, as they always do, mountains can't tell you what God has done about it. That's what the church is for."

My response was true, of course. But it totally missed the mark. It didn't reach people where they were; it didn't relate to their deeply held feelings about the church or their desire to know God.

For the "church is the mountains people," the organized church is, at best, irrelevant. At worst, it's a place they fear they'll find shame.

Churches teach that "the ground is all level at the foot of the cross," and that Jesus came "to seek and save the lost." But, at the same time, they give the distinct impression that a person must live as though he or she is *not lost* in order to be worthy of being sought and saved in the first place. One must wear the right clothes, ascribe to the officially approved beliefs, and enjoy only the "right kind" of fun. In other words, you need to be just like everyone else at church.

Similarly, the church proclaims that Jesus loves and accepts us "just as we are." But unless people are *like the rest of us in church,* we don't make them feel welcome and accepted. No wonder bar people often feel excluded from the church community.

This disconnect makes it easy for bar people to dismiss the church *and its message.* The church, as they perceive it, is simply irrelevant to their present and their future. They just don't want to be like us (as hard as that is for us to imagine).

Others, however, do show an interest in God, the maker of heaven and earth. My friend Ed (of the "Any damn fool knows there has to be a God who created all of this" fame) helped me realize that there was "another way home," another way of sharing the gospel of what God has done. A way already present and thoroughly in concert with our understanding of the God of creation.

In my experience of the Lutheran tradition, the Doctrine of Creation has become thoroughly overshadowed by the Doctrine of Salvation—so much so that we pay little attention to the former. "We behave," Pat Keifert said one day as we fished the Bighorn River in a drift boat, "as if God created us and the rest of the cosmos just so He could save it!"

But the truth is that God did *not* create us in order to save us! God created us in His image to live freely in the comfort and joy of who He made us to be, both as individuals and in community. He wants us to be comfortable in our own skins and to take joy in who we are meant to be as we live within His intent, as a new creation.

Many Christian traditions' strong emphasis on "matters of salvation" has led believers to ignore Scriptures like Psalm 8 or the creation stories in Genesis 1 and 2—in which God says of His creation, including humankind, "It was good."

This misplaced emphasis subverts the real, true goodness of the gifts God has given each of us, believer and non-believer alike. To those not familiar with our beliefs, it seems that the church teaches that there is zero goodness in any of us.

Consider this, for example.

Since the days of high school youth group, one of my favorite Bible texts has been something Paul wrote to the Galatians in the 5th chapter: "For freedom Christ has set us free, stand fast, therefore, and do not submit again to the yoke of slavery."

Years later, while researching the qualifications for being a lay leader in a denomination that emphasizes preaching God's grace through Christ, I found no mention of these leaders' being so *centered* in their identity in Christ that their lives fairly scream of the freedom in Christ to be the best "them" God has created and gifted them to be. Rather, the first qualification was that lay leaders be men and/or women who live "exemplary lives." Now, maybe those who developed the qualifications equate "exemplary lives" with "free, centered lives," but I'd bet you a nickel to a donut hole that this is not the case.

For most people, (both church and bar varieties), "exemplary" and "freedom" don't equate. Exemplary suggests living according to rules of conduct and displaying "proper" behavior. In other words, "We don't drink, and we don't chew, and we don't go with those who do." To some outside the church, this seems like the church's official motto.

Why is this?

Consider the mainstream media's coverage of American Christianity. The people who make news are the legalistic, control-hungry groups who declare that disasters like hurricanes and earthquakes result from God's wrath upon certain categories of "sinners"—especially those whose sin is "an abomination to the Lord."

Consider, too, the way churches treat some members of their own communities. When pastors fail in their personal lives—especially if that failure becomes public and involves sex—they are virtually crucified, without the benefit of a hearing before "Pilate."

When outsiders see how we "shoot our own wounded," it leaves an indelible negative impression—even if they believe the pastor in question did wrong and should face sanction. A church can say it's all about grace, but how it treats its members or staff in times of crisis betrays what's *really important*: Things like rules, judgment, and punishment

So what are we to do—if we do not wish to be seen merely as the arbiters of moral values in our culture? If we want to proclaim that God's primary intention for the world is *not* to punish it mercilessly for not toeing the line.

Maybe we can take a hint from the Wise Ones in the Christmas story who, being warned of dangers ahead, "went home by another way."

As we've seen, the contemporary church often oozes shame—shame before God and others. But this is not what God intended. God isn't the shepherd who searches for his lost sheep because that sheep has misbehaved and needs to be punished. He is the Good Shepherd who "seeks and saves" the lost lambs because those lambs are of great value to Him. He loves them.

Perhaps then, for the sake of the world that God loves, we need to actually listen to what those whose "church is in the mountains" have to say. Before we invite them to our churches, perhaps we should *go with them to their church* and worship God with them there. Worship without shame—although worship amid the mountains can certainly give a person a feeling of "smallness" in the grand scheme of things. But worship in nature is also usually marked by feelings of wonder, awe, and gratitude to the One who created it all. Such responses are good and true and appropriate in Christian worship. And they are accompanied by a sense of "fitting in" with what God intended for humanity from the beginning.

Those who worship in their "church in the mountains" experience a place where they *belong,* just as they are. They don't have to worry about whether or not they are welcome. They are a part of the world in which God, its creator, loves and values His creation.

Perhaps we in the church, whose evangelism efforts seem to focus *only* on human sinfulness and the (very real) need for forgiveness and reconciliation, are suffering from a lack of seeing the *whole* picture.

With most bar people, shame is something that manifests itself in their relationship with church people—or with the institution of the church itself. Shame is not part of their relationship with God Himself. Is it any wonder that they prefer to worship in the mountains rather than in church?

Common Ground and Going Home

Embedded in the biblical Christmas story is the tale of the Magi, the Wise Men who came to find the promised messiah. After seeking the advice of the religious leaders in Jerusalem, they do indeed find Jesus and kneel down in worship before

Him. When they leave, however, they are warned, via a dream, of the dangers of returning home through Jerusalem. Thus, they decide to "go home by another way."

What do you suppose would happen if, rather than trying to convince bar people of the *rightness* of our beliefs, their sin and need for salvation, we too tried going home by another way, beginning with the road they are on? What if we started by finding common ground—such as affirming our common understanding of God as creator?

We cannot, of course, ever neglect humankind's need for salvation. For Jesus came to seek *and save* the lost. *But we dare not forget why.* The Lord loves His creation. And if it is "in the mountains" where the segment of His creation known as bar people feel they "fit," maybe that's where we should go first. There, we can establish a relationship of trust that will lead to our being able to share how much God values His people, and how He has shown that love through Jesus our Lord.

If we do this—if we take seriously the bar people's spirituality and perspective on God—we will find that this "other way home" leads exactly where we wanted to go with them in the first place.

My old friend Ed is a perfect example. He shared my belief that God exists, but he didn't understand my "hang-up" with our need for a savior. But when his daughter died, he suddenly saw the reality of—and his need for—a God who is more than just a pretty good creator. Not because of any sense of guilt or shame, but because of his powerlessness in the face of death.

As I write these words, I'm still not sure if Ed "buys the whole package." But I know that when I shared with him (in terms he could understand and relate to) the hope of resurrection we have because of *Jesus'* resurrection, he was willing to start walking with me down the path. A path that goes home by another way. When I said, "You believe that everyone should know that God created us. Well, I believe that when someone dies, that same God can create him or her once again," Ed replied, with a glimmer of hope I hadn't heard in his voice before.

"You know, that makes sense," he said. "I'll have to think about that one."

I believe that the road Ed is on—a road that begins with his belief in God the creator, non-traditional though it may be—will take him home. I believe this because as Ed and I have walked together in this world, a world God loves so much, talking the way only two trusting friends can talk, I know we are not walking alone.

The Wonderful Problem
of the Freedom of God

"Yes, by and by. But first a larger matter.
I've had you on my mind a thousand years
to thank you someday for the way you helped me
establish once for all the principle
there's no connection man can reason out
between his just deserts and what he gets.
Virtue may fail and wickedness succeed…
…but it was of the essence of the trial
you shouldn't understand it at the time.
It had to seem unmeaning to have meaning.
And it came out all right.
I have no doubt you realize by now the part you played
To stultify the Deuteronomist
And change the tenor of religious thought.
My thanks are to you for releasing me from
moral bondage to the human race…
I had to prosper good and punish evil.
You changed all that.
You set me free to reign."
- excerpt from: Robert Frost, "A Masque of Reason,"
(God responding to a question of Job re: heaven)

IT'S ODD TO SAY IT, but it can be dangerous to give someone his or her first Bible. This is especially true if the recipient is a weathered, crusty 60-something rancher like my friend Ed, whom you should know fairly well by now.

If you were to sit at the bar and discuss religion with Ed, you'd appreciate the danger inherent in putting a Bible in this guy's hands.

Ed has shown a propensity for, shall we say, imaginative interpretation of religious texts.

For example, because Ed reads a lot, I once gave him a book titled *Religion & the Decline of Magic*. I thought its portrait of Christianity in Europe, before and after the Reformation, might be as interesting to Ed as it had been to me.

From the book, Ed learned about rural life for the average person in the Middle Ages and about how much of this illiterate population had come to view many Christian practices as magic. For example, the term "hocus pocus," originated in the Sacrament of Holy Communion, in which the priest "magically" turned the bread and wine into the literal body and blood of Jesus, while proclaiming, "*hoc est corpus* meum" ("This is my body.") The phrase was eventually morphed, by those unfamiliar with Latin, into "hocus pocus."

More significantly, it became the practice of some who took Communion to save the bread in their mouths, rather than consume it. They would then take the bread home and give it to sick family members, or even ailing farm animals, hoping that the bread's perceived magical powers would heal them.

Upon reading this, Ed theorized that sick people of this age would ask a priest to pray for them, lay hands on them, and give them Communion. Those who recovered became "true believers." If they died, of course, they wouldn't be around to tell anyone that the priests' efforts failed. Ed claimed that this was the reason Christianity "took hold in Europe."

"Christianity couldn't help but grow," he said, "if all that were left were the true believers!"

I never did understand how Ed arrived at this conclusion, but it shows how he was able to "tweak" what he had read, spinning the content until he had something he knew would get arise out of his "preacher" bartender.

Another example: Ed had learned that, prior to the invention of the printing press, monks hand-copied many old manuscripts, including the books of the Bible that had become accepted as "canonical." (The term "canon" refers to biblical content commonly accepted by the church as true and authoritative. These are the books that eventually made it into the "official" Bible.) Ed began calling these monks "Canons" and took delight in introducing me to Bull'n Bear newcomers by saying, "Jim here is a preacher, and he doesn't even know that the Bible was written by the Canons." I corrected him a couple of times, but soon realized that the truth wouldn't serve his purpose, which had nothing to do with who wrote the Bible or how it was transmitted. Why not let a guy have a little fun? We were in the bar, after all.

So you can see my "dangerous and hopeful" dilemma in giving Ed his first Bible. Who could know what he would make of it? On the other hand, I really had no choice.

It all started with Ed and me sitting at the bar one morning, discussing the previous night's Country Music Awards. I noted how strange it was to hear Elton John and Dolly Parton sing John Lennon's "Imagine" ("Imagine there's no heaven…") within 10 minutes of Brooks and Dunn singing about an old fellow who, after reflecting on his life, realized he needed to start paying more attention to the Bible's "letters in red."

"You know," Ed said, "I think it's time that I start paying more attention to those red letters myself." I could tell he meant it.

My task was clear. Ed had been my trusted friend for many years. In fact, I trusted him enough to let him sleep in the bar when he appeared in no condition to drive home safely. Though Ed truly liked his beer, never once in 15 years did he help himself to a brew before I came in to open the bar. Sometimes I would be greeted with a smile and words like "Man, am I glad you're here! I need some *medicine*."

Over the years, we had bantered back and forth across the bar about a lot of things, including religion. We had taken "road trips" together, to fish, to hunt, or to visit a bar in a neighboring town—for a change of scenery. Along the way, we'd laugh, swap stories, and rib each other.

Ed and I had traveled many roads together. The hardest one involved the death of his daughter Mary, whom you read about back in Chapter 6. This tragedy is what first turned Ed's heart toward those "letters in red."

Given all this, what else could I do but buy him a "red letter" edition Bible? That was the easy part. The hard part was thinking of what to write inside the front cover. "Good luck" wouldn't cut it.

When I sat down with what was soon to be Ed's Bible and started thinking about what to say, I found myself wondering about all the "church people" who already owned Bibles. Ed held strong opinions about these folks and how they did (or did not) follow the book's advice. Then my thoughts turned to the "bar people" who, like Ed, know only a few stereotypical things about the Bible.

Both groups' problem with the Bible, I decided was freedom. Not human freedom so much as God's freedom and our seeming desire to try to limit it.

Here's what I mean. Church people and bar people find it necessary to limit God and the freedom He offers, thereby trying to "tame" God. They want to create something they're comfortable with, something easy to handle. They define God as whoever they want Him to be. They "domesticate" God, keeping him in a box. They take God's own words, spoken to "the sea" from the book of Job, and try to use them on Him: "Thus far you shall go and no farther."

For bar people, this problem is a lot less complicated than it is for church people.

Bar people tend to define God according to their own ideals. Fairness is one of their core values, for example, so it is reflected in their belief that if the scales of Good and Bad tilt in the direction of the former, God will judge them "good enough." They'll go to heaven when they die. ("If there really is such a place," some are quick to add. Ed has harbored serious doubt about heaven.)

And what happens when the events of life seem to indicate God *isn't* fair?

The response is simple: "Who needs Him!?" At this point, some decide they'll "punish" God by refusing to believe in Him. You'll hear that in things they say like, "I just can't believe in a god like that."

For church people, however, the boxes we try to put God in have an origami-like complexity.

True, some of the containers are rather simple. *God is pretty much like I am.* Church people believe God shares their biases. Witness the people who protest military funerals, holding placards proclaiming things like "God Hates Gays!"

Or, consider how hard it is for many of us to hear God referred to as "She." God, of course, is Spirit, and the Bible uses both male and female imagery when describing the Almighty. But how many people still picture God as an elderly man with a baritone voice and a long white beard? (We will be well served when we can use the richness of both male and female pronouns for God, for then we will be able to incorporate a wider range of imagery and experiences into our relationship with Him, or Her.)

Now, on to those "origami boxes":

I know a young man whose sister was attending a particularly "holy" Christian college when she began having terrible headaches. Those at her school told her that, as a sign of her faith, she should refrain from seeing a doctor. She complied. Months later, when her illness became so painful that she desperately needed a physician, she was diagnosed with a tumor that had advanced far into her brain. It could have been arrested if detected and treated earlier.

Then, however, this young woman was told by her pastor that God hadn't healed her because her faith had not been strong enough. The pastor added that her mother's faith was wanting as well.

God "couldn't work," this family was told, because they hadn't "honored" God by demonstrating strong-enough faith. Their lack had rendered God *impotent*.

The next two and a half years brought several unsuccessful surgeries and rounds of experimental chemotherapy. All the while, this girl and her family were admonished that seeking these medical treatments demonstrated a lack of faith. God was testing their faith by withholding a cure.

Six months later, the young woman died. After her body had been in the mortuary for three days, someone from the church came to raise her from the dead. According to this person, "she almost came back," but in the end God said it was time to let her go—she was in His hands now.

I guess that God had finally escaped the complicated box these religious people had put Him in and was allowed to be God once more.

It's a problem, this limiting of God.

Without the Bible, God is limited by our cultural values or our sense of right and wrong.

Without the Bible, there is no room for God having the ultimate, self-defining word through Jesus, the Word made flesh. As we've noted before, you can learn a few things about God from creation, but you simply cannot learn about *Jesus* from the mountains or prairies or seas, no matter how much they say about God being a pretty good creator.

With the Bible, however, there are still risks. Such as our trying to tell God to go "thus far and no farther" by picking and choosing parts of the Old or New Testament. These parts become the "proof texts" to back up our viewpoint. We become "selectively literal" to prove we are right. In effect, we take God's name in vain by using some of His (or Her) Word to support our opinion—often against the witness of the rest of Scripture. And we limit God's activity in the world by trying to prevent God from being God—to be the One who has graciously and lovingly shown us as much as we need to see to understand how deeply He values us. (Though He has not revealed all there is to know about Him. Yes, God abides, but God also hides.)

The *surface* of faith in God, then, is that we believe He loves us and can do whatever we ask in Jesus' name. Jesus repeatedly encouraged this kind of faith.

The *essence* of faith, however, is to be found in trusting this God *regardless* of what He does or does not do.

No boxes.

No fences.

No puppet strings strung between God and us!

God *alone* is God. This is what the Bible Ed is going to receive says, and that is enough.

And so it is, with the problem of the freedom of God roiling and moiling around in my mind, that I came to know what to write in Ed's first Bible. After you read it, please say a little prayer for Ed, that through the work of the Holy Spirit he will come to understand and trust that the One spoken of in his new book is not only absolutely free, but is One who has freely chosen to be for him as well.

For my dear friend, Ed Weast

While this book contains those "red letters" you mentioned, it holds also stories about, and words from, those whose lives were forever changed by the one who spoke those letters in red. And though neither one of us believes that this Bible was literally written by the "hand of God," I do believe that it was written by ones who were both touched, and led, by that very hand. They believed that what they wrote was not only the truth, but was also true for them in the deepest sense imaginable. I believe that too.

I envy your eyes, Ed. Because you haven't read this book before, you will see things that my eyes do not; I hope you will share them with me. I hope also that you will get such a sense of what God can do (you will see that God is not to be domesticated and limited by the fences that either the church, or those outside of it, often want to build around him), that you will find wonder in what God did do. And in the end, I hope that this book will help you know not only what you have said that "any damn fool knows" (that there is a God), but that it will help you to actually know this God who already knows you.

Read well, dear friend. Wonder a lot. And give thanks for every time that what is true in this book seems like it might just be true for you.

Jim

"I Love This Bar!"

LET'S BEGIN WITH A POP QUIZ.

It came to me early one morning that a really good bar is like a really good church. As strange as it might seem, the best examples of these two institutions can be described by similar statements. As I thought about this, I couldn't help but smile. I toyed with the idea of a quiz, or checklist, to demonstrate the similarity.

By the time the morning sun finally gained full purchase in the big Montana sky, my mind had begun to catalog specific examples, such as the importance both church and bar place on hospitality to strangers.

Later, after an evening worship time down by Rock Creek, I asked my small community to help me add to my list. When they found out that this list was going to end up in this book, they started firing off statements, laughing and having great fun with the process. They took special delight when someone came up with a characteristic that should be a church's strong suit, but was usually exemplified better by the local bar.

Here is our list—and your quiz. Whether you are familiar with the bar, the church, or both, I hope that after you have checked all the boxes, you will have learned a few things you will find useful. (Feel free to check both if you think that applies.)

Church Bar

☐ ☐ This is where everyone knows your name.

☐ ☐ You wear nametags here.

☐ ☐ This is a safe place to be.

☐ ☐ Here you feel comfortable and accepted.

☐ ☐ Here you feel like you belong.

☐ ☐ You have fun with others here.

☐ ☐ Here you can be yourself.

☐ ☐ Here you socialize with your friends.

☐ ☐ Here you meet new friends.

☐ ☐ Here people take care of each other.

☐ ☐ Here you are not judged.

☐ ☐ Here the clothes you wear don't matter all that much.

☐ ☐ You meet potential "significant others" here.

☐ ☐ You tell each other jokes here.

☐ ☐ Here you can tell stories and laugh at yourself and each other.

☐ ☐ Here it's someone's job to listen to you.

☐ ☐ This place represents a wide variety of socio-economic classes.

☐ ☐ People expect God to be here or expect to meet God here.

☐ ☐ God *is* here or God meets people here.

☐ ☐ Here people sing songs together.

Church
Bar

☐ ☐ Here you can dance with your friends.

☐ ☐ People fall in love here.

☐ ☐ Here you watch people go through changes in their lives (terminal disease, marriage, death of a loved one, divorce, job changes.)

☐ ☐ People find a community that is supportive in all life changes.

☐ ☐ Here you have to "watch your step" so that you don't offend someone.

☐ ☐ Here people "have your back" if there's trouble.

☐ ☐ Here they collect money for services rendered.

☐ ☐ Most people come here on weekends; the more dedicated often come on weeknights.

☐ ☐ Here you must watch what you say, so that you don't get into trouble.

☐ ☐ Here people are tolerant of your opinions, and you can feel free to voice them.

☐ ☐ Here nobody acts like your mother.

☐ ☐ After an argument, people are less likely to hold a grudge here.

☐ ☐ There are parties here, both for special occasions and for no reason at all.

☐ ☐ Strangers feel welcomed and find new friends here.

☐ ☐ You're not alone here—unless you want to be left alone.

☐ ☐ People try to "fix" you here.

☐ ☐ What you receive here gives hope for when you leave.

☐ ☐ "This place is fun!"

☐ ☐ After their first time here, people want to come back.

Now that you've completed this quiz, are you surprised at the number of commonalities between bar culture and church culture? Were there disconnects that surprised you—things that should be a church's strengths, but are often done better at the bar?

Maybe some of you struggled with the quiz because you don't know much about what happens inside a bar. If that's the case, this chapter should give you a clearer picture of what happens inside the walls of a place like the Bull'n Bear. In doing this, I'm not trying to tempt you (especially you readers who are pastors) to start frequenting bars. My own little boat has encountered unruly rapids with the church over this matter, and I don't want to be responsible for launching anyone else down similar rapids.

Instead, I hope that pastors will view as assets those in their congregations who are already comfortable in the bar milieu. (There are people like this in almost every church, although they might feel that they have to keep this part of their lives well-hidden.)

If it is true that, in Jesus, God meets us just where we are, we must allow the disciples who know that particular "world" to say, along with other disciples in other worlds, "It is good, Lord, to be here."

Having said that, "Here's to the bar!"

With some exceptions, there are striking similarities between a good bar and a good church. In his song "I Love This Bar," Toby Keith sings,

> *"I love this bar, it's my kind of place /*
> *just walking in the front door puts a big smile on my face.*

No cover charge. Come as you are."
Here's a story that portrays what Toby means.

Hospitality to Strangers

Mikota is a Japanese-American who teaches at a large university's medical school. He's also an avid skier. A few winters ago, Mikota traveled 900 miles to Red Lodge for some skiing.

Upon arriving in town, after a day and a half of driving, he was hungry. He saw a poster in our window, promoting a half-pound burger and a "pound" of beer for $5.95.

Wow, that sounds good, Mikota thought. He parked his car, entered the bar, and ordered the "special."

Then he looked down the bar, noticing a long row of guys wearing cowboy hats. *Boy, am I in trouble*, he thought. He decided he should wolf down the burger and beer and get out of the Bull'n Bear as quickly as possible.

But before he was done, one of the "hats" got up and ventured to Mikota's end of the bar. He asked where the new-comer was from and what he was doing in town. The man's name, as Mikota would learn, was Eddie.

After the two had talked awhile, Eddie bought Mikota a beer. As it would turn out, this would be the first of many "free beers" Mikota would receive over the course of a long evening, courtesy of the friends Eddie introduced to him. ("They just kept buying me beers," Mikota explained to me later. "From then on, the Bull'n Bear was my bar in Red Lodge.")

Back at the university, Mikota now shares this story with all his classes (on the first day) to show his students the importance of making people feel comfortable.

Varieties of bars abound, but there are a few things basic to the trade. As Nancy and I tell every bartender who comes to work for us, "Most people don't come to a bar just to drink; most come to socialize." They come to be with their friends, or to make new ones. They come to laugh—and sometimes to cry in their beers. They come to tell their stories and hear the stories of others. They come to celebrate and complain. They come to relax after a hard day, or a hard week. They come to hang out with other people from their work-a-day world—but sometimes to escape that world, at least for a while.

"If Jesus were here today," I've been told more than once by those in the bar, "I think he'd hang out in a bar, rather than in the church."

It might surprise you that I've heard this comment from church people too. I think people from both groups realize that Jesus tended to hang out with the "kind of people" one would find in a bar.

But there are other reasons that some of my church friends have at least a few good things to say about bars. First, bars are often more honest places—in the sense that people can "be who they are." You don't have to be so careful about keeping up a certain image.

Also, there are no committees, something *many* church people find attractive (To paraphrase John 3:16, "For God so loved the world that He did not send a committee.")

In a bar, at least most of the time, no one is pressuring you to behave a certain way or support a particular political candidate or cause.

Finally, when a problem occurs in a bar, it's dealt with then and there and face-to-face. There's no place for being passive/aggressive or doing something behind someone's back. I've seen many conflicts end with the "winner" buying the loser a beer, and that's the end of it.

I should note that there is some biblical/theological support for the existence of a bar. (I mention the following examples *only* because they have all been said to me across the bar):

"Wine makes the spirit glad."—King David.

"Didn't Jesus turn water into wine after the wedding guests had drunk their fill?" (See John 2.)

And, of course, from the "wise" Benjamin Franklin, "Beer is proof that God wants us to be happy." (Ben Franklin isn't noted for having said much else about God.)

Is it any surprise, then, that when it comes to "just being myself and kicking back with friends," many church people tell me they prefer the bar to the church?

All in all, the bar seems to be a much less judgmental (and a much more accepting and relaxing) place.

You don't tend to encounter so many "raised eyebrows" in a bar. Yes, I've visited bars in which I couldn't be myself, places that made me feel unwelcome. But most bars I've visited are a lot like mine, and the experience in them is similar.

Having said all of this, however, we also need to explore what the bar is *not,* and for many church people, this shortcoming overshadows the positives.

What the bar is *not,* of course, is a place where real hope for our real lives can typically be found—at least not without God being present in the form of trusted bar-friends.

One of the bigger differences between the church and the bar is that, in the bar, life circles 'round and 'round the same old way. When all is said and done, in the bar, people experience pretty much the same old life, day after day after day. The same need for others, the same need to escape "real life"—or numb oneself to it. In other words, bar life is very good at occupying your time, but it won't give you time, especially time in the form of eternal life. Nor is the bar, as the church is, a place that promises to tell you how much God values you.

There is more the bar doesn't have: While it is a community and in many ways a very good one, it's only a limited kind of community. It is not the body of Christ. Yes, the bar serves food and drink, but these fill us only physically. One doesn't experience the true fullness of the bread of life that we receive, for example, in Communion.

And while God is present in the bar, He's often hidden. The bar is not the place where God has promised regularly to act openly among us, as He has promised to do in church, for example, in the spoken word and the Sacraments.

In the church, the hope we have in Christ is spoken openly. People walk in the doors expecting to experience that hope.

In the church, we hear of the new life God has accomplished in and among us. This new life happens day after day among those who are the church—right in the middle of that same old day-after-day life.

If all of this wasn't so, I'd simply stay in the bar all the time; many of my best friends are there, and it is, we must not forget, also a part of the world God loves.

But it is so. And because it is, I am in the bar not only because of my friends, but also for a different reason. The same reason (I literally hope and pray) that Jesus went to "those sorts of people" in "those sorts of places": To bring the hope and peace of God to bear in the everyday lives of people I have grown to love—when the time is right. I am in the bar because I enjoy the people. I am in the bar also because this is where God's mission has taken me.

Jesus really was a friend of sinners, and He really did enjoy being with them wherever they were, establishing His kingdom there too, which, like every good church or bar, really does invite people, "Come as you are."

The Attack of the Bible Thumper

"We have met the enemy and he is us."—*Pogo*

MY GOOD FRIEND ED was waiting for me on his favorite bar stool the other morning as I unlocked and entered the back door of the Bull'n Bear. He was there from the night before. (As I've mentioned, he sleeps on the couch upstairs if he's "too tired" to drive home safely.) When he heard me enter, he swung around on the stool and said, "Where were you when I *needed* you? I got attacked by a Bible thumper yesterday! All I did was mention that I had just started reading the New Testament and off he went about the way he thought I was supposed to understand and believe in it. He even went and got his Bible out of his car. It had footnotes and cross-references and explanations in the margins, and he nearly beat me to death with the fool thing. "

This episode was quite a setback for poor Ed. In the Bible I gave him, he had already "gotten through" the Gospels and Acts. He was working on Romans when "Bob the Bible Thumper" attacked.

Now, to remind you, Ed is a weather-worn, set-in-his-ways rancher who didn't own a Bible until he was 64. After he had begun reading the New Testament, he would come into town, have a few beers, and give me his take on a recently completed passage. Sometimes he taught me something. Sometimes he delighted me. Other times he just made me shake my head.

"What's God got against pig farmers, anyway?" he asked one day—referring to Jesus' dispatching demons into a herd of pigs. The pigs, you may recall, then rushed headlong into the sea, where they drowned. Given his occupation, Ed sympathized with the poor farmer who owned all of those pigs. "Raisin' pigs ain't all that wonderful in the first place," he observed, "without having some overly zealous religious guy run 'em off and drown your whole herd!"

Other times, though, Ed was serious about what he'd read. As you probably recall, he received this Bible after his daughter Mary died at age 33. He had decided it was time for him to "pay a little more attention to those 'red letters.'" Mary's death was real hard on him.

I wonder if Bob the Bible Thumper would have treated Ed differently if he'd taken the time to listen to his story. To discover why Ed was reading the Bible in the first place. Like a growing majority of Americans, Ed was never instructed in the matters of the Christian faith. He was never taught any doctrine, much less "correct" doctrine.

I hope the time will come when Ed is ready for some doctrinal instruction, but what he needs *now* is not an officially approved understanding of the Christian faith, complete with footnotes, cross-references, and marginal notations.

Ed needs peace.

He needs peace in the face of his daughter's death—and at the prospect of his own. The peace that accompanies finally knowing the One who knows him best. The One who has the power to give the life Ed so dearly needs.

In short, Ed does not need proper teaching *about* God. He needs to be gently introduced *to* God, his maker and redeemer.

Unfortunately, most of us in the church are more adept at (and more comfortable with) "instructing in" rather than "introducing to." Why is this? I'm afraid that too many of us have a closer relationship with *what* we believe than with the One in *whom* we believe.

As the comic strip character Pogo said, *"We have met the enemy and he is us."*

Christians have, after all, spent the better part of the past few centuries defining and then protecting the particulars of what we believe. This is especially true within certain denominations. The result, I fear, is that we have become communities of shared doctrines more than communities of people who share a *relationship* with God; Christians whose identity is derived from being "confirmed in" our faith, rather than being *transformed by* our faith. Or, rather, transformed by the One who is the object of our faith.

It is no wonder, then, that so many "evangelism programs" have fallen flat, with both the evangelizers and the would-be evangelized. If sharing one's faith is "one beggar telling another beggar where there is bread," the hungry ones aren't likely to be too impressed by someone boasting about her favorite recipe for marble rye. A recipe doesn't do much for an empty stomach.

But "beggar to beggar" no longer describes the sharing our faith. Church people seem more intent on telling bar people what they need to believe *about* God rather than introducing them *to* God. Bob the Bible Thumper, for example, seemed to care little about whether Ed *knew* Jesus. He was most intent on persuading Ed to adopt certain beliefs *about* Jesus.

If only church people, and the bar people they seek to influence, could get back to basics. Faith, as the Bible describes it, isn't in any *thing*, like a doctrine or creed. Faith is trusting in our risen Lord, even when life doesn't make sense, even when the Lord Himself is beyond our understanding.

This truth was recently brought home to me in a delightful way on Pentecost Sunday, at one of our "crossing the bar" worship services down by the creek behind our house. Cindy, a faithful member of our little community, posed a question she had been wrestling with since the beginning of her faith journey. After hearing the story of Pentecost in Acts 2, she said bluntly, "I don't get it. What is faith?"

I responded, "Having faith in God is the same as trusting God."

"Faith is *trust*?!" she replied. "I've worried that I didn't have enough faith, because there's so much that I don't know, but I *trust* God."

I was both dumbfounded and encouraged in my own faith. Cindy has been through incredible hardship in her life. Looking at her, one could see both the truth and the irony in the fact that we sometimes show *greater* faith when we question and doubt than when everything seems to make sense to us. For it is in times of doubt that all of our reasoning melts away, and we find ourselves having to let go of our own devices and simply trust in the One who says that, no matter what, we can trust Him with our lives and the lives of those we love.

This is where peace is finally found, in a relationship with the God who loves us enough to come after us. Many times, this is all that church people need to share with bar people.

One beggar telling another where there is bread.

A mother or father singing "Jesus Loves Me" with the children.

A friend telling a friend who is having trouble, "This is what has helped me and given me peace when I was going through the same thing you are."

A bar owner telling a patron/friend of the hope that keeps him afloat, no matter how unruly life's waters become.

A few Christmases ago, Cindy and her husband, Bubba (a very large and equally kind and gentle Native American man), attended our annual holiday campfire down by the water. It had been the first time Cindy had joined us, and she told me that she and Bubba "really enjoyed it."

Less than a year later, right before Christmas, Bubba suffered a major heart attack and was suddenly gone.

When I saw Cindy late that same winter, she was nervous and crying. She told me she wanted to ask me a question. She wanted me to explain why God had taken Bubba from her.

I explained, as plainly as I could, that death was not God's "gift" to the world; death comes from another source. God is about giving life, even though death steals it from us for a while. That answer was hard for her. Indeed, for most of the "hard-living," understanding God's sovereignty in all things is vital to helping them cope with life's struggles.

A few months later, Cindy, now tending bar for me, asked a couple more questions.

The first was about the Lord's Prayer. "What does that word 'hallowed' mean, anyway?" she wondered. This was followed by another question about the prayer: "Is the Lord's Prayer really the *only* way we are supposed to pray? I think even God would get bored with that." She laughed nervously as she added, "I know I do."

I gave Cindy short answers to both questions, but I don't think I provided what she was really after.

Cindy had lost her husband. They should have enjoyed decades together which were stolen away from her. She wanted to talk to God about it, but she wasn't sure how. She's wasn't even sure if God comes close enough to listen. But she needed to talk to Him.

Do you see? She didn't want to know about prayer. She wanted to pray.

She, like Eddie, didn't want to know about what the peace of God is. She needed the peace itself.

She wanted more than knowledge *about* God. And it's important to note that as she has lived and struggled and grown in her trust of God, her knowledge of Him has increased. But that knowledge followed faith, not the other way around.

As a trained and educated pastor, I could have answered—using sound theology—a good number of Cindy's questions about God. But I've found deeper joy in joining with our faith community to introduce Cindy to God and walk beside her as that new relationship put down roots and, eventually, gave her wings. Cindy's faith relationship and all that follows it will reveal the answers to her questions. The One she has come to know will provide them.

Where Cindy will go from there, only God knows. She's okay with that, because she trusts God. And God will give her peace along the way. I'm pretty sure of that.

At least that's what he's done for *this* beggar.

FREEDOM AND THE CHURCH OF THE ULTIMATE

I REMEMBER TELLING MY MOM and dad a "crossing the bar" story about my exploits as a preacher-turned-bartender. I don't recall the precise details of the story, but I do remember my mom being the ever supportive mother. She noted, "I suppose good can be done even in a place like that."

My dad, ever the traditionalist, said my story was just another attempt to rationalize my being somewhere I shouldn't be in the first place.

Dad wasn't trying to be unkind. He wasn't even being insensitive. He was an honest man, but he was kind as well. He was merely telling the truth as he understood it. He really cared about matters of faith. His own faith had sustained him as he grew up with a father who was a binge-drinker. My dad's family ended up losing their farm during the Great Depression, but my dad didn't lose his faith.

During World War II, while serving in Belgium, he stepped on a land mine and was seriously wounded. Again, his faith sustained him.

Later, as the father of five children, my dad looked to God to give him perspective and guidance. He was determined to share the faith with others, especially his family.

So, you can see where my dad was coming from when he critiqued my occupation. He, too, had been stung by the "unruly rapids I went through in my marriage," he too felt shame, and he feared that my Bull'n Bear venture was yet another willful step down the wrong path. In his view, I was "in the world" *and* "of the world."

It was Dad's well-considered view that the Kingdom of God shouldn't contain any saloons. I don't share that opinion, but out of respect, I never argued the point with him.

My dad died suddenly the day before his 81st birthday, and in the years since, I've found myself recalling that "crossing the bar" conversation with him and my mother. My dad was a self-disciplined man in all areas, including his faith. He lived out his life with a sincere gratitude for what God had done for him. He didn't feel he had to "earn his way" into a relationship with God. He knew he already enjoyed that relationship. His actions were simply a way to say thank you to God.

I remember one time when dad came home from the golf course to tell us that he had shot a hole-in-one that evening. It is the custom among golfers that anyone who accomplishes this feat buys a round at the club house bar for all who are there. Given dad's feelings about the abuse of alcohol, it was a tough thing for him. He bought the round, but didn't have a celebratory drink himself, and clearly had mixed feelings about it all.

Unfortunately, many of the people my dad encountered misunderstood why he lived his life in such a way. They thought he was living by a set of rules mandated by his faith. They didn't understand that the gospel had freed him and he *wanted* to live according to what he believed was right. To be sure, he regarded himself as a sinner—but a *forgiven* sinner, eager to please God with his life.

By now you know I have no trouble speaking a "word against" church people who say that following the rules is what matters (especially those who impose this philosophy on others). But I want to distinguish this group from people like my dad, who work very hard to live a worthy life but do it, not out of compulsion or even a sense of duty, but out of their thankfulness for the grace they live under. I deeply respect these people.

I *do*, however, want to tell these people that many bar people don't see their underlying motivation. Thus, they get lumped in with all the other "legalistic Christians." If we are serious about bringing reconciliation and hope to the world God loves, which includes the world of the bar people, we must change this perception.

Throughout this book, I have emphasized Jesus' being the "friend of sinners"—about His coming to "seek and save the lost." I've also written about how we who are the church are called to participate in fulfilling God's mission. To do this effectively, we need both a better understanding of the *free-*

dom we have in Christ, and the determination to live our lives on the basis of it.

As they strive to help the gospel cross the bar, churches must finally recognize the assets they have sitting among their congregations (probably in the back rows, trying to look inconspicuous). These "unexpected children of God," as I call them, most likely already have relationships with bar people. And rather than criticize those among us for frequenting local saloons, we should encourage them, teach them, and free them—with our blessing—to represent the body of Christ, even in a bar.

Before unleashing these "unexpected children," of course, we need to deal with the church's interpretation of being "in the world but not *of* the world." Traditionally, this axiom has meant "setting a good example" or being the keepers of the public morality.

Ironically, this interpretation, which most of us grew up with, has actually made the church *more* like the world, not less. Let me explain: Consider how many politicians view the church's role in contemporary culture. We're to be the rule-enforcers. Hence the term "keepers of the public morality." To some, the church is the arm of a political party. So, while we have been called to preach (and to live out) the wonderful message of the gospel, our rich calling has been reduced to something much less.

If you question the truth of the previous statement, ask yourself this question: Do most people (both church people and bar people) equate Christianity with a set of rules for proper behavior or with a freedom enjoyed through Christ?

On a similar note, what is more important in how the church evaluates its leaders: their moral behavior, or their ability to live their lives according to the freedom they enjoy through Christ that it is evident in the love they have for others?

Please understand, I'm *not* saying that behavior is unimportant. Quite the opposite is true—for individuals, churches, and denominations.

How we live is *deeply* important. Our behavior determines how the bar people will hear and respond to the gospel message we share. But instead of focusing on being slaves to the Law, our lives should reflect the freedom God has given us—including the freedom to be the friend of "sinners."

Freedom, however, is not what my bar-people friends believe the church is about. To them, Christians are the ones who proclaim *how* people should live, not *why*. They don't hear about the freeing, unique-to-Christianity gospel and what it means.

To be "in the world but not of it" or to "live a life worthy of your calling" does *not* mean that we are placed back under the law. It means that death no longer has the final word and that we no longer have to live in fear. We are "born again." We are "A new creation." Paul said it clearly to the church at Galatia (in Galatians 5): "For freedom Christ has set you free. Stand fast, therefore, and do not submit again to a yoke of slavery."

Paul addressed these words to believers who wanted to require circumcision (which was part of the Jewish law) as a prerequisite to becoming a Christian, making following the law a way of earning the right to receive the *free* gospel.

Today, the church often tries to do the same thing. Because they rarely see the freedom and hope we have as followers of Jesus, to the bar people the call to "follow Jesus" is merely a call to follow a bunch of rules—new versions of the same old rules. So much so that when they do see Christian freedom lived out among them, they don't know what to think of it.

Let me give you an example.

Buck, a 58-year-old customer and friend of mine, describes himself as a "hundred and twenty dollar a month cowboy." Imagine one of the hired hands from an old western movie, and you'll have a pretty clear picture of Buck.

When Buck was growing up, going to church meant that his mom scrubbed his ears on Saturday night and twisted them on Sunday mornings—when he misbehaved during the service.

Church was part of the routine for moms and kids like Buck, until they reached 6th grade or so and got to stay home on Sundays to help their dads with "the chores." Though Buck's dad was himself a strictly religious man, Buck grew up in a culture where church was pretty much for women and children.

"As I grew up," Buck says, "I *knew* the difference between right and wrong; I just liked some of that wrong stuff a whole lot more! I s'pose that's why I've been married four times."

Buck can go on for hours with stories about his life, and it's always entertaining to hear him describe the trouble he's gotten himself into—and out of.

"I was married to a Las Vegas hooker once, for *three* days," Buck told his audience at the bar one night. "She was 'Miss February' on a pin-up calendar, and I had her autographed picture!"

"It went missing, though," he added with a frown, "after I married my *next* wife."

Buck is quick to point out that his romantic exploits were all in his "younger days." "I've got a good one [wife] now," he'll say, "and I'm not about to mess that up by 'chippying around'!"

From all appearances, Buck and his wife do have a wonderful marriage. They've been together for a long time now, and show no sign of faltering.

One day, however, after Buck had told a group of us about his growing up knowing the difference between right and wrong, he turned his attention to me.

"But *YOU*! he said with an accusing tone, "You were a *preacher*. You're not s'posed to be in bars and playing poker and drinking whiskey!" I sensed that he was implying, as my father once had, that my credibility as a Christian witness was undermined by my lifestyle.

Buck had a strong opinion of what a Christian was (and was not) supposed to look like. I didn't fit the bill.

He had never learned how one's relationship with God can set him or her free in surprising ways—even the way that leads through the back door of a saloon. You never know where the joyful pursuit of life with God can take you.

Buck's attitude has made it hard for me to take the freedom and joy of the gospel "across the bar" to him. Like many in our culture, Buck defines Christianity as a system of proper behavior, not as a freedom born of gratitude to Jesus for what He has done.

Maybe this attitude is so entrenched because rules are cut and dried. You either follow them or you don't. Rules make it easy to judge who is living right and who is not.

Freedom, however, is fluid. It flows from the wellspring of grace; it goes wherever it needs to (and *is needed*) that it might serve God's mission. Freedom allows people to be comfortable in their own skins as they, with God, build a relationship with their Creator and those He created. They don't have to "be circumcised"; they don't have to look and behave exactly like everyone else.

This is the message that we ought to be preaching; this is what is ultimate. Though how we live our lives morally is important, especially because Christian morals are grounded in love for God and our neighbor, it should and will always remain secondary to that which is *ultimate*: the saving, vast, and wondrous message of the gospel of Jesus, which sets us free as children of God.

What does this mean for those of us who strive to cross the bar?

For one thing, we need to strike a blow for the freedom of the "unexpected children" of the gospel. Their lives may not match our culture's Christian stereotypes; they are following Jesus' example as the "friends of sinners." They should be allowed to expect and receive God's blessing. They should also receive the church's blessing for their efforts, for they are in just the right place to tell their friends why they trust in God and what that has meant for them.

I'll say it again: How we live our lives—as individuals and as the body of Christ—is indeed important. We should never fail to live lives worthy of our calling. But let us hold tightly to what's *ultimate*, the "why" behind living worthy lives. We have been reconciled to God through Christ and sent out to bring the ministry of this reconciliation to the world. We should live and move with the joy and freedom that are part and parcel of being members of the kingdom Jesus is ushering in. This is why we exist. This is the calling we share.

We should never settle for presenting a Christianity that lacks the grace and freedom Jesus brings to our lives—that is, a Christianity overflowing with rules and demands. For if we settle, we will be unfaithful to the Lord's call to go into *all* the world, a world God loves, bearing the hope and freedom that are the essence of that which truly is gospel.

Krissy, Tigger, Jesus and James Dean

I HEARD A STORY about a kind and well-loved priest who stood at the gates of heaven after his death. How deeply this priest had loved God was evident in how well he had loved his congregation, and he was greeted at the gates by Saint Peter himself. Peter asked the new arrival if there was anything special he wanted to do in heaven.

The priest thought for a moment before saying, "Is there any place where all the things our Lord said are written down, just as He spoke them? I'd love to read them all. I have so many questions."

St. Peter told the priest that heaven contained a complete archive in the main library. He led the priest there.

The priest sequestered himself in the library, and Peter didn't hear from him for almost a year. Then, one day, he heard a loud scream coming from the library: "Nooooooo! It can't be! It just can't be!"

Peter ran into the building to check on the priest asking "What's wrong?"

"There's an 'R'" the priest cried, in horrified disbelief, "an 'R'!"

"What do you mean?" Peter asked.

"It says CELEBRATE," not celi*bate*!" the priest said.

One day, Nancy sat at the bar with her friends Kathy and Marsha. I wasn't there, so I can give you only a second-hand account of the conversation, but apparently the subject of guilt feelings came up. Kathy noted that you can't let your life be run by guilt, to which Marsha, raised as a self-described "good Catholic girl", replied, "If it wasn't for guilt and being afraid of God's punishment, everyone would do whatever they wanted to."

Hmmm . . .

Another conversation:

Several weeks earlier, my friends Steve and Rob and I were talking at the bar about Rob's upcoming wedding. Steve turned to Rob and said, "You should have Jim here do your wedding."

Rob and I were both embarrassed, but Steve continued, undaunted, "You know what I like about Jim? He isn't one of those ministers who think you have to, like, totally dedicate your life to God. Are you, Jim?"

I immediately thought about Jesus' many comments on the subject. Finally, I offered, "Well, it all depends on what you mean by 'totally dedicate,' I suppose."

Then Steve came up with this zinger: "I don't think that God even *wants* you to dedicate your whole life to Him."

Hmmmm . . .

Steve and Marsha are an interesting pair.

Marsha seems to perceive that what God wants is "right behavior" from us. That behavior is coerced out of us by guilt and fear. Guilt and fear, administered through the church, are God's preferred ways to keep us all in line.

Conversely, Steve seems to think that God isn't all that concerned about our "total dedication" to Him. (By "total dedication" I think he means: "Don't do the 10 things you want to do and *start* doing the 10 things you don't want to do.")

In Steve's eyes, God gives us, as we say out west, "lots of rope."

Enter Kristine Walker Todd.

How can I describe Krissy?

A few years ago, Krissy tended bar part-time at the Bull'n Bear. She was friendly to all and full of life. She also suffered severe mood swings. She could go from lighting up a room to brooding darkly in a corner. I once described her as "a wonderful cross between Tigger [from Winnie the Pooh] and James Dean." Everyone laughed in agreement.

One slow night, she plopped down on a barstool next to me. She regarded me with sparkling eyes and said, out of the blue, "I believe in Jesus, you know!" She then went on to tell me that she had been baptized when she was little, and that she knew she belonged to God.

Krissy lived with a man she loved named Rick for several years. Rick had proposed to her many times, to no avail. Then, in the throes of one of her "up" moods, Krissy finally said yes (even though he hadn't been asking her at the time). Not only that, she informed Rick that I would be performing the wedding—which was to be held in the upstairs ballroom at the Bull'n Bear. Their friends and family would be there, she said, especially their fellow Harley-riding friends.

On the wedding day, Krissy showed up 40 minutes late. Rick and I stood around waiting for her. He shrugged his shoulders and smiled, as if to say, "Well, what did you expect?"

When Krissy finally arrived, I asked the guests to set down their drinks and take a seat.

I began by reading the creation story from Genesis, then the story of Jesus' miracle at the wedding in Cana at Galilee. I shared with Rick and Krissy God's intention for them from creation. I reminded them that God's image existed in them, even today.

I emphasized God's desire to have a continuing presence in their lives.

Krissy thought Jesus' miracle at the Cana wedding—changing water to wine—was pretty cool. She said so, right out loud during my sermon. It was a wonderful day.

Two years later, back in the Bull'n Bear ballroom, I read that same Genesis creation text (in which God, seeing all that He had created, said "It was very good), but this time I was reading it at Krissy's funeral.

When it came to Harley riding, Krissy's joyful attitude was, "You can't feel the wind through your hair if you wear a helmet." On a ride one warm spring afternoon, she apparently hit some gravel while cutting a corner a little too sharply. She lost control of her Harley and crashed head-on into a guard rail.

These words were printed on the back of Krissy's funeral folder:

"Life should not be a journey to the grave with the intention of arriving safely in an attractive and well preserved body, but rather to skid in sideways—cigar in one hand and vodka squirt in the other—body thoroughly used up, totally worn out and screaming, 'Whoa, what a ride!"

Three people:

Marsha, who would describe herself as a "church person."

Steve and Krissy, both devout "bar people."

Each held a different view about what God intends for our lives. Each exemplified, in his or her unique way, something I learned a long time ago:

There is great confusion, both within and beyond the Christian community, over what God has intended for humanity from the beginning.

Marsha spoke for many church people and bar people when she said, "If it wasn't for guilt and being afraid of God's punishment, everyone would do whatever they wanted to."

If the church has successfully promoted one thing, it's that God is deeply concerned about what we do. Sin, then, is more narrowly viewed as doing things that are wrong. It's not "missing the target" of becoming who God created us to be, of living out His plan for us, nothing more and nothing less.

For his part, Steve doesn't think God cares much about wrongdoing or missing targets. I don't think he's ever even wondered much about what, if anything, God wants for us.

It all makes me wonder . . . maybe Krissy was onto something in the way she virtually exploded into life, striving always to be the "best Krissy" she could be.

She was aware she needed forgiveness for her sins; she told me so, during the same conversation in which she told me she believed in Jesus. She knew that Jesus freely granted that forgiveness, simply because He loves her. She told me that too.

But beyond what she told me, I sense that Krissy found peace in something most of us have forgotten—that God's unconditional grace is not something we need only after we're dead. Grace frees us, each and every day, to be fully alive, to be who God meant us to be. To live a life based *not* on fear and guilt, but on our love for God and His people. To possess a joy for life that any good father or mother would want for their child.

Jesus came to "seek and save the lost" and called all of us to "go and make disciples." As church people strive to answer this call, how much more effective do you think they'd be if their joy and gratefulness over being God's children outshined their desire to get the bar people to behave properly?

This Christmas, after we sing carols together, hear the Christmas story from the Bible, and discuss the precious gift that Jesus is to us, I'm going to remind our little community of something we often forget, even at Christmas: One of the gifts that God wants to give each of us at Christmas is *ourselves*! The wonder of everything our loving God intended us to be.

The freedom to explode into God's life for us. After all, if God had wanted us to be someone or something *other* than who we are, He wouldn't have made us *as* we are.

One of my seminary professors, Gerhard Forde, once said something that changed my life from that point on. "Jesus," he said, "was in many ways the only true man who ever lived, because He didn't try to be anything other than who He was." With this in mind, as we pray around the campfire, my prayer for each one of us will be that we, too, will seek to be nothing more, but nothing less, than who we've been created to be. This, I believe, is not only what God wants *of* us; this is what He wants *for* us.*

* The full text of Krissy's funeral sermon is printed in the appendix.

MILK FOR FREE

AS I WRITE THIS, I am 57 years old. My children think this makes me an official "old guy." I've got an "Old Guys Rule" T-shirt to prove it. My friend Buck, who wonders how he got over the hill without ever being on top of it, tells me I'm still just a pup, even though he is only two years my senior.

Whatever I am, I know I'm in that time of life when one laments how few things he is be certain of. It's hard to find anything I can say without hastily adding, "On the other hand . . ."

On the other hand, (see what I mean?) aging does bring with it a few realizations that make you shake your head over why they took so long to sink into your thick skull.

I have been involved with the church for most of my life. I was baptized when I was two months old, sang in the "Cherub Choir" as a young child, and did the whole Sunday school/Confirmation/Youth Group thing. Then I went on to a Lutheran college and later to seminary. I served as a pastor and performed concerts in hundreds of churches. I was thoroughly "churchy." And I loved it. Not like one loves a favorite music group or hit song. I loved the church like a child loves his parent.

I wish, though, that it hadn't taken me so long to see what it truly means to be part of a church, the way that Cindy does. Church means so much to her. She longs for our worship times. Her life benefits from it, and it shows.

Recently, my friends Pat and Breda (both teachers and leaders in the church and the world-wide missional church movement) worshiped with us bar people at one of our campfires by the creek. They saw in us a community of both the happy and the broken, the single, the married, and the widowed. They saw some who are struggling with serious health problems, including substance abuse problems, all gathered together around the good news of what God has done, and is still doing, in our lives.

Pat and Breda saw people laughing and singing together, praying for each other by name, and listening to a Bible text—followed by a short message about God's intent for us and how much He values us. They then listened as those around the campfire talked about where their lives had been and what being part of our community means to them.

Pat and Breda shared with us the bread and the wine of the Lord's Supper. They sang with us, and saw how our lives were intertwined with one another, through Christ

My two friends saw a young church that moved them and gave them a sense of hope about the church around the world. Many there were both surprised and encouraged when, asked by one among us if they had anything to say, Pat told us as he spoke, "You are the body of Christ."

"Wow!" Cindy said.

Before our campfire services began long ago, I had an inkling of what church could be. But none of us had imagined it could be like *this*. Some in our community had seen the various forms of church and had decided this particular institution was not something they wanted to be associated with. Part of the problem was that church was seen as a place people went, not something you *are*.

✻　✻　✻　✻　✻

There is a saying I first heard as a teenager: Why buy the cow when you can get the milk for free?

Oddly enough, this old adage represents many of my non-church-going bar friends' attitude toward the church, God, and salvation.

More on this later . . .

✻　✻　✻　✻　✻

Terri was still developing arms and legs in her mama's womb when her older brother Michael was killed in a tragic accident at the family home. He was three years old.

One day, Michael's father, relaxing in a living-room chair after a long day at work, asked his young son to close the screen door, located off of the kitchen. (This was the kind of door that featured a sliding glass panel that could be moved to cover the screen.) When Michael reached up for the door handle, a sudden gust of wind caught the door and slammed it into him. The glass shattered, cutting Michael so badly that he eventually bled to death—despite frantic attempts to save him.

Terri's dad never forgave himself for "causing" his little boy's death by being "too lazy" to get up and close the door himself. Neither did he forgive God, who "commands the wind and the waves."

I do not know how this family's Lutheran congregation responded to their tragedy. I don't know if the family were active members in their church or not. I do know, from Terri, that Michael's death is the reason she and her younger sister had never been baptized—as Michael and another older brother had been.

After all, Terri's parents reasoned in the midst of their shattered emotions, why entrust your children to a God who would allow a tragedy like Michael's? Terri also told me that after Michael's accident, her father self-medicated by drinking until he eventually drank himself to death.

*　*　*　*　*

Cliff grew up on a ranch in eastern Washington, "far away from everywhere that was anywhere," as the saying goes. He is not your stereotypical eastern Washington rancher. Cliff is in his mid-40s now, but looks much younger. In fact, the first time he came to my bar and ordered a Crown and water, I carded him. "You're kidding me!" he said, handing me his driver's license. He was 42 at the time. I bet he still gets carded a lot.

Cliff served his country in the armed forces in the first Gulf War. Twice he was wounded by enemy bullets. He once told me that his military experience "cured me of any use for religion."

During poker games, Cliff likes to bum cigars. He typically smokes about half an inch of a stogie, and then puts it aside. (This has often irritated me, as I'm the one he usually bums cigars from, and when I smoke, I smoke pretty good cigars.)

One time at the poker table, Cliff told me he had been sent away to a Catholic boarding school, which he attended from "when I was little, all the way through eighth grade." From his tone, I could tell that he did not recall that time with any fondness.

Later, at another poker game, held after Nancy and I had announced our intentions to sell the bar, Cliff asked me, "So what are you going to do next?"

I hesitated before answering. I didn't know how he would respond. Finally, I told him that I was going to perform church concerts—as I had done before—and that I was intending to write this book, and hopefully do some speaking along with my concerts.

Cliff regarded me with that signature twinkle in his eye.

"Just what would *you* (a bar owner)" he laughed, "have to say to people in church?"

As an answer, I offered up the unique perspective of a preacher who had also owned and operated a saloon for 15 years. Cliff turned dead serious. "Wait," he said, "you mean you're going to go back to preaching against people?"

Preaching *against* people. This response caught me by surprise.

"Preaching is supposed to be *for* people, not against them," I said.

"That'd be nice for a change," he said. Then another hand was dealt, and the conversation moved on to other things.

*　*　*　*　*

Still a red-headed fireball in her mid-70s, Holly attended the Bull'n Bear's "Old Friends Gathering" one Sunday afternoon. We started talking, and she asked me cheerfully, "What have you been up to today?"

I mentioned that I had sung in church that morning.

"Oh. I don't go to church anymore," she informed me. "I don't believe in *any* organized religion."

"Well what do you believe in," I replied, "*un*-organized religion?" I immediately knew it was the wrong thing to say. I braced myself for her response.

"You don't tend to go back to church," she said, burning with an anger that had been simmering for five decades, "when the pastor, *using your name*, accuses you personally of certain sins right from the pulpit during the Sunday morning sermon." She gathered herself before adding: "I *believe*; I just don't believe in *church*!"

*　*　*　*　*

A recent poll indicates that the fastest-growing religious group in the United States is those who claim "no religious affiliation." I bet that a good number of this group have stories like Holly's, Cliff's, and Terri's.

And I imagine that this group also has its share of proud "rugged individualists," who are plentiful here in the American west.

This brings us back to our saying "Why buy the cow . . ." Here's how that saying relates to the church: Bar people reason, "If God is good and loving (i.e., fair)—and if our souls live on after we die—why would anyone waste a perfectly good Sunday morning hearing about a bunch of rules based on how the church wants me to live?"

Or to put it even more bluntly: "If our salvation is *free*, as church people claim, why tack on the 'cost' of church?"

"Why buy the cow—and deal with all that responsibility?" (Most people around agriculture know that cows need milking twice a day, *every* day. Even Christmas.)

This philosophy took center stage when I talked with Terri about being baptized.

I raised the subject during an Easter campfire worship service after Terri had said to me, "I've believed in Jesus for just about as long as I can remember, and I have always wanted to be baptized. It just never happened. First, because of what happened to Michael, and second, I suppose, because I just wasn't very interested in the whole 'church' thing. But I'd like to be baptized."

Nearly a year passed. Then, before the next Easter campfire service, Terri approached me again about her desire to be baptized and I agreed that I would baptize her on the upcoming Easter Sunday, down by the river where we worship.

But then I ran head-on into a major problem. It was like hitting a wall.

The "wall," in this case, was my friend Pat Keifert, seminary professor, founder and head honcho of Church

Innovations. After I told him about Terri's upcoming baptism, Pat delivered to me a firm and emotion-filled pastoral
word:

"If you're going to do this," he said, "you'd better finally
get serious about starting a real community—a church—for
Terri to be a part of, because you know she won't go to any of
the other churches in town."

I knew that he was right. I also knew that my concep-
tion of "church" had been woefully inadequate.

You see, every day at the bar I converse with people
who view a relationship with God as deeply personal and
private. Research done by Church Innovations bears this out
as a widespread viewpoint.

Also, I have noticed that the average bar person sees a
relationship with God as more about the future, *not* the present. God is like the fire extinguisher stored behind a pane of
glass. It's to be broken Only in Case of Emergency. Like that
fire extinguisher, God's presence provides a measure of comfort, but He's not intended for everyday use.

Pat helped me realize that it would be a great disser-
vice to Terri if I allowed her to treat her baptism as something between only her (the individual) and God—a source
of "personal and private" comfort. Baptism *is* personal, of
course, but it's much, much more.

In baptism, as the apostle Paul said, we are joined to the
death and resurrection of Jesus, and to the church, which is
His body. I've always believed that Paul meant what he said
about baptism. I just haven't always acted like it, and now
what had been lacking in my attitude toward baptism and the

church was as obvious as a cow standing in the middle of a flock of sheep.

After Pat and I finished talking, I felt like a weight had been placed on my shoulders rather than the joy I should have been feeling over Terri's upcoming baptism. The negative church-related experiences of many of my friends—combined with my own experiences and hang-ups—had seriously skewed my understanding of what the body of Christ, and baptism into it, truly is.

Pat was right. Right in what he said, and right to say it. Although, at the time, I would have preferred to remain "in the dark."

Our conversation got me thinking more deeply: Having Jesus as our *savior* is not just a theological point, it is our most desperate need—a need we cannot meet any other way. And none of us would either know or experience the gifts we receive by being part of the body of Christ if it weren't for the church.

This means that the "milk" we get for free is not just salvation; it's also the wonderful privilege and responsibility of being joined with others as we live out that free gift—every day from now to eternity. It is a gift wrapped in the relationships we were created to be a part of. A relationship with *God,* but also relationships with the *entire company of saints* who have been redeemed and sent into the world by God.

So, to apply "Why buy the cow when you can have the milk for free?" to the Christian life is foolish. It's like asking, "Why waste time enjoying a good, loving, and ever-deepening relationship with your spouse when your marriage license says he or she is already 'yours?'"

The problem for the church, however, is that its people often represent it as solely a source of laws and demands.

This problem can't be blamed on the faulty perceptions of those outside the church. If we tell the truth right out loud about the message we give to those "outside," we must confess that we present ourselves more as a judgmental "religious club" than as the body of Jesus—as ones who live life the way He did.

Yes, our good motives are honorable. And, yes, a church needs structure and organization. But we are seen primarily as a religious machine trying to influence—or even regulate—how our neighbors behave. (And too often shame is our No. 1 tool.) We are not seen as people who proactively accept and love our neighbors the way Jesus did.

Many people don't "see" their local church and the joy we have in being a part of it. They see Organized Religion, which is, at best, boring, and, at worst, a threat to their freedom and enjoyment of life.

✧　✧　✧　✧　✧

After my conversation with Pat, I went back to Terri, to talk again about baptism and all it means. When she told her fiancé, Richard, what we were discussing, his joking response was "Yeah, Jim will probably tell you to start going to church or something."

I have since told the two of them that Richard was right, just not as he understood it. Church is not someplace you go; it's what, by God's grace, you *are*.

After the Easter service that saw Terri baptized down by the water, we gathered around the campfire and discussed "being the church." We agreed to "get serious" about meeting regularly (not just on Christmas and Easter). We now meet every other week, an unlikely group of people in an unlikely place who are the body of Christ.

After all, why settle for just the milk, when you can have the whole cow for free?

MARVIN'S GARDENS

As Jesus died on the cross, one of the thieves
being crucified with him, pleaded, *"Lord, remember me when you come into your Kingdom."*
Jesus replied, *"Truly I say to you today,
you will be with me in paradise."*
Jesus' response to the thief recalls parable of the
lost sheep (recorded in Luke 10). At the end of the parable, Jesus notes that "there will be more joy in heaven
over one sinner who repents than over ninety-nine
righteous persons who need no repentance."

DESPITE OUR EFFORTS to put life into "good order," it
remains anything but tidy.

We fret over our mistakes, and we're often even more
upset about the things we *should have done* but didn't, for
whatever reason.

When my friend Marvin died a while ago, one of his
childhood friends confessed to me after his funeral, "I knew
Marvin all my life, and I'm a Christian. But I never said anything to him about it [the hope Christians share]."

If Marvin Kivikangas, whose story I am about to share,
could have looked down from heaven at all of people who

attended his funeral, he probably would have fallen right out of heaven itself. He never knew how well he was loved.

Marvin knew lots of people and seemed to be congenial with all of them. He was in the middle of many bar conversations, a mug of Bud Light in hand. However, he had few, if any, true friends, the kind of friends who would invite him to go fishing on the weekend.

Once, the 60-something Marvin told my wife "Ya know, I should have gotten married,—dammit, but I never got around to it." (Meaning absolutely no disrespect, Marvin often punctuated his statements by saying "dammit." As you will see, he never gave it a thought. It was just his way.)

Marvin had a lot of people who would ask him, "How are ya doin'?" And they cared about his answer. But none of them actually got involved in what he was doin' or involved him in what they were doing.

And so it came to be that Marvin's funeral was standing-room-only, though his life was marked by loneliness. Many times during his visits to the Bull'n Bear, he'd tell Nancy, "It'd be better if I was dead." He hoped, I suppose, to get a reaction out of Nancy—which he always did. "Marvin," she would tell him, "that's not true! We love you, and we would miss you."

I first met Marvin back in the early 1980s, while I was still a pastor. He was a backhoe operator for the city, and he dug and refilled graves at the cemetery. Thus, our occasional encounters were at funerals.

When people talked about Marvin, they would observe that he "wasn't the sharpest knife in the drawer," but these observations were free of malice. Even as a youth, Marvin was known as "slow;" however, he had a knack for remembering exact dates of specific events in Red Lodge. No one else in town could touch him when it came to this kind of recall.

After Marvin's funeral, a man approached me and shared this story: Marvin was raised in a home in which only Finnish was spoken. He went through kindergarten, first and second grade before any of his teachers discovered he could speak English! I suppose he had enjoyed the extra attention this had given him from his teachers, though he got in trouble when he was found out.

Since he had never married, Marvin lived with his mother until her death and remained alone in that house until he died. He had a good job working for the city, plowing snow, repairing streets, and digging graves. He stuck with his job, retiring at age 62, when he could receive his pension.

At the funeral, Skip, Marvin's foreman from work, shared how Marvin was always careful and respectful as he dug and refilled graves. Because of the effort he put into his work, the Red Lodge Cemetery came to be known by the city crew as "Marvin's Gardens." "What was planted there was planted with care," they said.

Marvin was just a casual acquaintance to me while I was a pastor. I obviously came to know him better after I bought the Bull'n Bear. The bar was where I first heard the famous "Marvin" laugh."

This laugh started out low, like an air-raid siren just getting cranked up. Then it became higher-pitched and increasingly intense until—at its peak—it culminated with a staccato blast of "aw-aw-aw-aw," coming from the gut. So it was that when Marvin laughed, everyone laughed. One didn't need to hear the joke or comment that started it all. Marvin's laugh, all by itself, was absolutely delightful and irresistibly infectious.

One cold and snowy Red Lodge night, Marvin had consumed a few too many beers to safely drive his pickup home. I offered to give him a ride. When I dropped him off in front of the berm of snow that he, no doubt, had created when he plowed the streets that day, I drove away, never giving a thought to whether he would be able to get over the snow and into his house.

He wasn't.

The next morning, an injured Marvin showed up at the bar. He had been to our local clinic, and the doctor there told him he needed to go to the hospital in Billings for further treatment. He asked me for a ride, holding up his hands to show me why he couldn't drive. He had fallen in the snow and had trouble getting back to his feet. During his struggle, his fingers had become frostbitten. He wasn't in danger of losing any digits, but they were badly blistered. They looked like sausages that had been cooked so long that they were ready to burst.

I loaded Marv into my old '76 Ford F-150 pickup, and we headed to Billings. During the drive, Marvin recalled that I was once a Lutheran pastor. He told me that his parents were Finnish Lutheran but never attended church. Thus, he had never been baptized. His parents, I think, were Lutheran much like they were Finnish—by accident of birth, not effort.

"I know about Jesus and all that,—dammit," he explained, "and it bothers me that I never got baptized." He told me that he believed in Jesus—and that he knew that baptism was "something you were supposed to get done." He seemed truly upset that his parents had neglected this.

I told Marvin that I'd be happy to talk with him further about getting baptized. We ended up tabling the discussion until later—as getting treated for frostbite was a more urgent matter at the time.

Years passed, and I brought up the subject of baptism up from time to time, but Marvin would always defer the discussion "until later." So Marvin's baptism became one of those perpetually "undone" things we end up feeling bad about later.

"Later," in this case, ended up being July of 2009— 15 years after I first re-encountered Marvin at the bar—as he lay in a hospital bed with a severe case of pneumonia. Marvin's niece Marcy called me one day to tell me that her uncle had been in the hospital for a couple weeks, but he had received almost no visitors. She requested that I visit him. I agreed, and for some reason, told her the story of Marvin's perpetually delayed baptism.

Marcy was silent on the other end of the line.

"I never knew that Marvin's mom never got him baptized," she said, finally. I could tell she was crying. "Would you talk with him about that again?"

I visited Marvin the next day. We shot the bull for a while, and then I asked if he'd like to discuss baptism again.

"Well," he answered, "later on maybe. I'm feeling pretty good right now,—dammit. They haven't got me in the ground yet! I may pull out of this yet,—dammit."

And that was that. Or so I thought.

A couple of weeks later, Marcy called me again. Marvin's doctor had informed her that her uncle had only about 48 hours to live. She asked me again about the baptism. I confessed that I hadn't made any progress last time, but I promised I would go to the hospital immediately and talk with him again.

Nancy and I headed to the hospital right away. En route, we called Kathy to see if she could join us, but we couldn't reach her. We called Richard (Terri's husband) and left a message on his phone.

I was hoping that at least a few from our little "church by the river" community could join us for the baptism—assuming Marvin would allow it. I believe strongly that baptism is not just a private thing. It is a "body of Christ" thing. Sadly, it didn't seem like I was going to be able to contact anyone on such short notice. Then we passed Kathy going the opposite direction in her car. We flagged her down and explained the situation. She told us she'd drop everything and join us. When we arrived at the hospital, we saw Richard pulling into the parking lot behind us. He'd received our voice mail and headed straight for the hospital in Red Lodge.

Once inside the hospital, a nurse informed me that Marvin had been given small doses of Atavan and morphine to help him deal with his anxiety. When we entered his room, we found Marvin sitting up in bed and eating spaghetti. Limp noodles dangled from his mouth.

We visited for a while, and then I told Marvin that it was probably time that we revisit the subject of baptism.

"I've asked Nancy and Kathy and Richard to come along," I explained, "just in case you wanted to be baptized. You're not alone in this. They've all been baptized into Jesus too."

While Marvin continued with his spaghetti, I read from John 3—the story of Nicodemus coming to Jesus at night, and Jesus talking to him about being "born anew." I ended with John 3:16. From there I explained what baptism was all about. I asked if Marvin believed that Jesus was sent by God to bring us all back to God.

"Oh, yeah, I believe that," he said.

I went on to tell him that being baptized meant he was joined to Jesus' death and resurrection, that all of his sins were forgiven and forgotten by God. And I told him that because of Jesus, a person doesn't have to worry about what happens after death, because God has promised us we can be in heaven with Him forever.

"So," I said, "do you think you'd like to be baptized today?"

"Well,—dammit, maybe later," Marv answered. "When I'm back on my feet."

I could not believe my ears.

"Well Marv," I responded, "I'm not here to push you into this. I just thought it might give you some comfort while you're so sick, because you told me once that it kind of bothered you that you hadn't been baptized."

He was silent for a moment that was clearly uncomfortable for him. Then the conversation moved on to other things. After a while, we departed, wondering if we'd see Marvin alive again.

As we exited down a hallway, Nancy stopped.

"I wonder if Marvin was embarrassed about not being able to stand up," she said. "Maybe he thinks you have to stand in order to be baptized."

"Why don't I go back and ask him," I said, recalling how Marvin hated to feel embarrassed.

While the other three members of my group waited outside, I re-entered Marvin's room. I told him what Nancy had said.

"Oh no," he said, "It's not that. I just thought I could do it later. I think I've got the sleeping sickness or something; I'm so tired all the time."

"Marv," I said, "you're sleepy because they've given you medicine to make you not so worried. Don't you remember the doctor telling you she didn't think you would be getting better? Marvin, that's why Marcy asked me to come up here and ask you if you'd like to be baptized right now. There might not be very much 'later' coming your way."

He was silent for a moment, letting it all sink in.

"Well,—dammit," Marvin Kivikangas said finally, "I suppose I ought to get it done now then."

This declaration—and the way he said it—surprised me, but not as much as what Marvin said next:

"*How much does it cost?*"

I smiled an incredulous smile. Marvin, who was always a little strapped for cash, was worried about how much baptism cost.

"Oh Marv," I assured him, "it doesn't cost you a thing! The price into heaven has already been paid for you. That's what Jesus is all about: He paid with His life to bring you home to God."

"Well then—dammit, let's get it done."

So, with water from a small disposable plastic cup—and the promise of the Lord of heaven and earth, Marvin was baptized in the name of the Father, and of the Son, and of the Holy Spirit. Joined to Christ and to His body forever.

After we were done, I reminded Marv that if he ever got scared, he could look back on his baptism and remember that God had promised that no matter what happened he would be okay, because God had made him His own.

About a minute later, in the middle of my saying good-bye, "the sleeping sickness" kicked in and Marvin fell asleep.

The next day—while I was fishing with my friend Jack—Marcy called and left a message on my phone. Marvin had died at 3:00 that afternoon. His last words to her, said with a clear and sincere sense of peace, were, "I got baptized, you know."

At Marvin's memorial service, I told the overflowing crowd gathered to honor and remember him the story I've just told you.

I told them, too, the story of the cross on which Jesus died next to a thief; where from that high vantage point He fulfilled the simple and profound promise of a searching God…finding.

At the cross, we see the power of that promise—the promise that one day we will laugh and rejoice with the angels in heaven. And somehow, above all that heavenly mirth, I expect to hear Marvin's peculiar laugh rising above the crowd, as it always did, bringing yet one more round of laughter.

Tumbling

IT HAS BECOME INCREASINGLY ODD to me how different are our *perceptions* of reality versus actual reality. I know that "we do not see things as they are; we see things as *we* are," but the contrast goes deeper than that.

Twelve miles south of Red Lodge, Highway 212 starts its winding way up Beartooth Pass, which Charles Kurault once called "the most beautiful highway in America." As you make your way up the pass and look to the right, you can see, thousands of feet below you, Rock Creek, the flowing stream of water that eventually flows behind our house. That creek has given me countless hours of enjoyment—fishing; sitting with my wife in lawn chairs, having a cold brew while the cold water washes over our hot feet on a summer day; singing and talking and worshiping with my friends from the bar; or just enjoying the solitude of a random evening.

But I have never (until now) stopped to consider how, up the pass from our home, one unique snowflake is joined by other unique snowflakes, in accumulated depths of 100-plus feet in some places. This yearly phenomenon is not only what allows for farmers and ranchers to irrigate their crops down in the valley, it is also what eventually allows me the pleasure of the little creek behind my house. A single snow-flake, which I give no thought, is a necessary reality for the existence of the creek—to which I pay great attention.

As I've shared before, Nancy's and my first years of operating the Bull'n Bear were marked by frequent prayers of, "Please, dear Lord, get us out of this bar!" And this prayer was to become a running tradition for the next dozen years.

For many of the first 10 years, Nancy and I covered 11 of the bar's 14 weekly shifts—on top of parenting small children and other responsibilities. It was hard work for meager pay, and it might have been more tolerable if either of us felt we belonged at the Bull'n Bear. For that whole time, however, the job didn't seem to be a good fit for either of us. While I welcomed the chance to occasionally share some hope with those who seemed at the moment to be particularly short of it, I often wondered if I was using these "ministry opportunities" to rationalize being where I did not belong as my father had once suggested, and being stuck in a place I didn't want to be.

"*Please* send someone to buy the bar!" was a frequent prayer for Nancy and me—to which we would graciously add, just in case God didn't do it, "if it is your will."

"No," seemed to be God's consistent answer. Apparently, it was *not* His will.

This brings me back to this chapter's first sentence: Our perceptions of reality often have little to do with reality itself. In this case, our present perception of what we thought surely must be within God's will for us (getting us out of the bar) was different from what God's future held for us, as was evidenced by keeping us there.

Today, looking back over the past 15 years, Nancy and I can see that we have been deeply blessed. We've lived in an unusual world—especially for an ex-pastor—but we know God loves this world *and* that the bar is part of the world God loves. We have come to love and respect the people in it.

We feel we now belong here more than any other place, and are grateful and privileged to take part in this part of God's mission. We didn't always see what God was up to in all of this, but He has been, all along, gracious enough to give us glimpses of His purpose. Many of these "glimpses" are the stories shared in this book. Stories of crossing the bar.

Epilogue

ON A RECENT FRIDAY NIGHT, Nancy and I went down to the Bull'n Bear to "have a few" with our friends. After 15 years, we had finally sold the bar, and the new owners had declared this particular Friday one of their TGIF party nights. They hired a band and even put out some snack chips and those little cocktail weenies bathed in barbecue sauce (the ones that always smell way better than they taste).

Shortly after we arrived, Cindy (who has become our dear friend) led us over to an older gentleman she introduced as her "former boss" Stan. As Stan and I firmly shook hands, he looked me straight in the eyes and said, "I want to thank you for all you have done for Cindy. You and Nancy have really made a difference for her."

Cindy, I later learned, had worked for Stan as a heavy equipment operator shortly after her husband, Bubba, died. Stan had witnessed the raging waters Cindy had been thrown into, at a time when she had no understanding of God's grace or the reality of the gospel.

Later that night, Cindy told Stan of the first "Christmas campfire" she and Bubba attended. She recalled how they stood together, gloved hand in gloved hand, hearing how God had come to be with all of humankind. How they sang songs proclaiming the miracle of that first Christmas long ago. I didn't know it for a long time, but that night was a treasured shared memory for Cindy and Bubba.

After Bubba died, Cindy moved from their home on the Blackfoot Reservation near Glacier National Park to Red Lodge and began working for us at the Bull'n Bear. Soon, she began asking questions that had been forced to the surface by Bubba's death.

She wondered if there would be more campfires, and she eventually became instrumental in my scheduling regular services at "the church by the creek."

By the water, we worship a lot like God's people all around the world. But we also have a drink or two, and we make sure we spend time talking about life's hard questions. Questions that must be asked, but have a hard time being voiced. (It is often the case that the real questions people want to ask aren't ones that they dare ask in church.)

Through it all, Cindy's life has slowly and subtly changed direction as she has come to know the God that Jesus described in the parables of the lost sheep, lost coin, and lost son. The "looking for the lost" God who is also the "finding and rejoicing" God.

Of Cindy's many dilemmas about God, one of the most memorable to me was revealed when she shared her distress over the fear she could never love God as much as she still loved her late husband. She felt she might be "in trouble with God" because of this. She was greatly relieved to hear that since God created in us the need for relationships—and the ability to love—He would probably understand that the mere presence of her concern was evidence of her love for God, and of her desire that this love would grow.

Cindy still has all of her wonderful "Cindy-ness" as Stan would say, but she has changed. She has begun to see how she has a part in God's mission.

At one of the campfires, Cindy shared how much she still missed Bubba. She said, (without, I am positive, ever having read the opening sentences of Paul's 2nd letter to the Corinthians), "Well, maybe God can use me to help comfort others whose husbands die, 'cause I know what it's like."

Here's another "glimpse into God's purpose": I still remember the look on Kathy's face as "the lights came on" when we discussed "sin" around the campfire one night.

Sin, as you might imagine, isn't a popular a topic with bar people. They feel like they are "object lessons" when church people teach their children about sin. (e.g., "Kids, don't grow up to be like *that!*")

You see, for people with little or no contact with the church—or who have somehow been burned by the church—a word like *sin* immediately produces feelings of shame, shame that they are unacceptable or even worthless in the eyes of the church and perhaps even in God's eyes. I've heard it hundreds of time from bar people: "The church doesn't want people like me."

So I told our little group by the campfire that the Greek word translated in the Bible as "sin" (*ha-mar-ti-a*) was most widely used in that culture as an archery term for "missing the mark," or missing the "bull's-eye." That explanation *hit* the mark with our group. And just as I had hoped, we started talking about the "bull's-eye" in relation to our lives before

God. I could almost see the light bulbs clicking on above their heads.

"Maybe the bull's-eye isn't a bunch of rules at all," I offered, "but rather what God intended us to be when He made us." And with that, as they say at the race track, we were off.

We talked for a while about "missing the mark" in life, and what that looks like. Then the discussion quite naturally moved toward Creation. Was God talking about people too, someone wondered, when He looked at the world He had made and said, "It is good"? After all, fish swim. Birds fly. Horses run. God made us to be who we are, and intends something for each *of us* as well, something *good*.

As we continued, I could sense the simple wonder over the realization that *each person* is valued by God. God loves His world and each individual in it, including all of us in our little church. (We covered a lot of ground that night, hopping from sin to creation to the value of the individual to the church. It is startling when we remember that this was a group of bar people, sitting around a campfire, with drinks in hand.)

At one point, Kathy interjected, "But we screw it up. Maybe that's what sin is. Nothing more than we don't want to be what God meant for us to be."

"And it's killing us," I added. "For with sin came death. That's why we need a savior."

From here, we tumbled on, to the foot of the cross and the opened tomb; to what God has done about humanity's straying from His intent for our lives.

So it went. One campfire and one group of bar people—who are also *God's people*—talking and wondering together, and getting ever closer to the freedom given us by the gospel. And it all happened in the midst of God's creation. It was good.

It's been more than six years now since Eddie, who referred to me as a "damn fool preacher" the first time we met, suffered the death of his daughter Mary. By the time of Mary's death, Eddie and I had come to know each other pretty well. But when I tried to offer some hope to him, he said, as you might recall, "There is no hope. Mary's dead, and I've just got to get used to it." It cut me to the bone to see my friend in such pain—and utterly without the hope I took for granted.

A month or so went by before we talked more about Mary. But one day, as we walked along the bank of Red Lodge Creek, I asked him "If God can create a first time, why couldn't He create the same thing a second time? That's pretty much what the resurrection of the dead is." I thought this question might connect with Ed, as he has always acknowledged that there is a God. (You can't see a calf being born or a ewe lambing without knowing *that*!" he was fond of saying.)

Ed thought about that question. I believe he's still thinking about it, as evidenced by his vow to "start paying more attention to those letters in red." And since his recent heart attack—and having been "shocked back to life," all this before he learned he had cancer—I know he's starting to realize that God wants him around for some reason. Some unfinished purpose. He's even talking about getting baptized and "making it official."

And he's not the only one.

Mickey, a former Marine (though it appears to me that one never stops being a Marine) once endured chemotherapy for intestinal cancer. Now he's suffering from an unusual type of hernia, located high in his abdomen, the result of having been shot in battle. A while ago, he was invited to our little church by the water. There, he was welcomed and accepted. We worship with him and pray for him.

Just like we prayed for Peggy who (though she never was a drinker) had liver cancer and fought it with all that she had in her. Her husband, Barry, was included in every one of our prayers for Peggy, because he loves her and has struggled with her cancer in his own way. Peggy helped us wonder together about things that everyone else wanted to talk about—because everyone wanted to know what God was up to in all of Peggy and Barry's struggles. Peggy died recently, and Barry remains in our constant prayers, because he still has many battles to fight. Cindy thinks she should talk with him about what is getting her through it all.

John, meanwhile, kicks against God at every opportunity, often expressing his anger at how his life has turned out. But he still comes to the water to worship, nearly every time we meet. Lately, he's been bringing his young adult son, who has his own questions and observations that are openly welcomed.

Terri was baptized on Easter Sunday a couple years ago. She and Richard were married the following August, and the two of them are reveling in the new direction their lives have taken. After a long period of avoiding worship (I hope to tell you someday about Richard's devastating journey in a cult-like religious group, which left him deeply antagonistic toward anything "church"—every Christmas he would wear a T-shirt emblazoned with the words "bah humbug," and he meant it!), they now invite people—usually while in the bar—to the campfires. These two invite others to "church" more than anyone else I have known—including during my time as a pastor.

Nancy has no idea how important her hospitality in our home (and all the work that it has entailed) has been to the advent of the Kingdom of God in this place. She would, no doubt, object to my saying anything about it in this book, but it is wonderfully true. Her "preparing the way of the Lord," and her hospitality to friend and stranger alike has made a huge difference in the work—the mission—that God is accomplishing here.

Now, if you had told me in an earlier season of my life that I would be a part of stories like these, I'd have taken away your drink and said, "Don't you think you've had enough?" But life does tumble to places we might not have thought we'd go—often to places we absolutely *did not want to go*. Still, I have learned this lesson well: Wherever God's mission takes us, we do not go alone, even though it sometimes seems that way.

Even though they regard God differently, bar people and church people alike often seem to go through life with a kind of *practical atheism* when it comes to their perception of

God's active involvement in this world. Most people I know believe that God exists ("any damn fool knows that…") and that He can do whatever He wants. Most even concede that God made Himself known in the past (in Bible times, for example), and that we will meet Him, somehow, after we die.

Unfortunately, these folks don't seem to be aware that God continues to be active *right now*—every day. He didn't "retire" after the Bible was written. Just as Christmas, in all its wonder, proclaims, God is still with us. These years in the bar have taught me that.

This reality is part and parcel of the wonder of being part of the church. If we believe that we are sent to a certain place (even a bar), it's because Jesus Himself wants to be there. (See Luke chapter 10.) Jesus wants to be with us wherever we are, here and now! We are never alone, never on our own. We journey with God, who is still up to something in this world, a world He values and loves.

Once in a while, when the spring run-off from the Beartooth Mountains is particularly strong, even the large rocks in Rock Creek are moved by the force of the current. The sound the rocks make—as they tumble along, crashing into each other—is amazing. It resembles distant artillery fire.

After a week or two of this phenomenon, the creek bed itself is changed. You can see dramatic shifts in the currents, in the water's direction and flow. New fishing holes, runs, and riffles emerge. There are new places to ford. The old creek has been re-created by forces God began long ago in creation, leaving once more something new for us to sit by a campfire and regard with wonder.

It's hard to imagine that a single, gentle snow flake that fell in the mountains the previous December had a part in all of this new creation—happening far, far downstream. But, together with thousands of other snowflakes, it most certainly did. And it is very good.

Appendix

The story in Chapter 13 contains portions of Krissy's funeral sermon. Our community was, as you might imagine, shaken to the core by Krissy's untimely death, for it is rare that someone comes along who simply exudes life the way that she did. At her funeral, the ballroom of the Bull'n Bear was filled with bikers and bar people. I knew going in that almost none of them held any positive regard for religion or religious services. They were there for Krissy and Rick, not to hear any preacher rant, or bore them to death. It was to this congregation that the following sermon was preached.

Funeral Sermon for
Krissy Walker-Todd
June 28, 2008 (Krissy's birthday)

Genesis 1 (selections)—In the beginning God created the heavens and the earth. The earth was without form, and empty, and darkness was upon the face of the deep; the Spirit of God was moving over the face of the waters. And God said "Let there be light"; and there was light. And God saw that the light was good...

...and God separated the waters (above) from the waters (below),

...and God said "Let the dry lands appear ...and let the dry land bring forth vegetation," and it was so. And God saw that it was good.

...And God said, "Let there be lights in the heavens to separate the day from the night, a greater light to rule the day, and a lesser light to rule the night...and stars also...and it was so, and it was good.

And God said let the waters and the dry land bring forth living creatures, each according to their kind, and let them be fruitful and multiply, and it was so, and God saw that it was good.

Then God said "Let us make man in our image...so God created man in his own image, in the image of God he created him; male and female he created them. And God blessed them...And God saw everything that he had made, and behold, it was very good.

Romans 6: 3-5. "Do you not know that all of us who have been baptized in to Christ Jesus were baptized into his death? We were buried therefore with him by baptism into death, so that as Christ was raised from the dead by the glory of the Father, we too might walk in newness of life; for if we have been united with him in a death like his, we shall certainly be united with him in a resurrection like his."

Greeting: Beloved of God, grace to you and peace from God our Father and our Lord and Savior Jesus Christ. Amen.

I heard a story about a kind and well loved priest who had died and was standing at the gates of heaven. That he had loved God much was shown it by how well he had loved his people. St. Peter himself came to greet him, asking if there was anything special the priest would like to do, now that he was in heaven.

The priest thought for a moment and then said, "Is there any place where the words of our Lord are written down just as he spoke them, word for word? I'd love to read them all, I have so many questions."

St. Peter told him that they were indeed all recorded and archived in the main library, and took the priest there.

After not hearing from the priest for the better part of a year—he was enjoying himself so much—all of the sudden there was a loud scream coming from the Library...

"Noooo...It can't be. It can't be!"

Peter runs in and asks the priest what is the matter.

"There's an 'r,'" he cried, "an 'R'."

"What do you mean," Peter asked?

"It says "CELEBRATE," not celi*bate*!"

I know of very few people who, without too much in the way of selfishness or doing so at the cost of others, mastered the art of being—of CELEBRATING—who she was made to be better than Krissy, and when we say we are here to celebrate her life, we do so knowing full well that we are second in line behind her. She did being Krissy very, very well, giving thanks to her creator through the simple act of being who she was, without pretense.

Krissy Walker-Todd, daughter of God. Most often happy-go-lucky and bouncy, sometimes brooding, she was like some wonderful combination of Tigger from Winnie the Pooh and James Dean.

As is true of all of God's creation, God made something "good" when He created Krissy. The value that she had and *still* has in the eyes of her Father in heaven—again, this is true of every one of us—is greater than what even those of us who tend to think about such things can ever imagine.

It is because of this great value, of course, that I can think—and speak—about Krissy as I do. For in saying that she was very good at being who God created her to be, I don't mean that she did everything right, made all good choices, and never "missed the bulls eye," so to speak, of being who God intended her to be. No one save Jesus alone can lay claim to that, and she knew it full well. She knew she was in need of God's grace and forgiveness just like all the rest of us.

What I *do* mean, however, is that because of the great value in which her heavenly Father held her and holds her still, she received that grace and forgiveness just like she received the wonder of life itself, with arms wide open, and a heart grateful that God's arms are wide open for her as well.

I know so because she told me so.

One day while she was working a bartending shift for me at the Bull'n Bear Saloon, quite out of the blue—she did this, I suppose, because her boss the bar owner was also her boss the pastor—she said "I believe in Jesus, you know!" She then went on to tell me that she had been baptized when she was little, and that she knew she belonged to God.

I believe that it was with *that* on the inside that she was able to "do Krissy" so well on the outside. And so she was...

Krissy Walker-Todd, daughter of God; created with gifts and detriments, loves and dislikes, things which haunted her and things for which she deeply hoped; sometimes brooding, but more often bouncing high above it all.

Now I don't know if she ever thought about this, because we never talked about it, but the way Krissy so freely did who she was created to be—joined together with her belief in what God had done for her in Jesus—almost makes me think that she somehow knew deep down inside of herself what it is that so many others have either forgotten, or never knew in the first place. And what is that?

It is that when God created us, God had in mind who God wanted us to *be* much more than God had in mind what we were to *do*.

Our life in this world, and with God, was never created to be and was never meant to be judged simply by whether we do the right things and don't to the wrong things (and then try to have fun).

Our life in this world, and with God, is finally to be lived based, not on *how* we are (in terms of how we follow all the rules), but on *who* we are, which is inseparable from *whose* we are. There *are* those who try to follow all the rules—Krissy didn't work too hard at that one—but it is our relationship with *God*, not our relationship to the rules, that is finally what it's all about, and that comes only as a gift from God, who alone can give it. We can never earn it or deserve it. We simply live within it. And not just when we die, but every day that we live as well.

Krissy knew that love of God, that her heavenly Father's arms were always open to welcome her and strong enough to hold her safe even through the day when she would die (as will each one of us), and she fairly exploded into life in the comfort and safety of that belief.

Somehow, though I don't know whether she talked about it with others as she did with me that one day, it is my belief that this is what lay beneath and behind all the wonderful ways in which she was Kris.

Krissy Walker-Todd, daughter of God; That's probably not something she would have put on the back of her leather jacket as she headed down the road, but it *was* something which she held in her heart and freed her to be the Krissy we knew.

And it *is* something that will carry her all the way beyond her death to a resurrection like Christ's and home to the welcoming and waiting arms of her Father, who gave her life in the first place, the wind to blow through her hair, and has promised to raise her, to re-create her life, yet one more time.

It is what God said he would do, and as we have seen from the very beginning, when God speaks, it is so! And it is very good. Amen.

AfterWord:
AN OUTSIDER'S VIEW

by Breda Ludik

BREDA LUDIK is Pastor for Worship and Research at Helderberg
Dutch Reformed Church in Cape Town, South Africa and a part time
teacher in the theological seminary at the University of Stellenbosch.

✻ ✻ ✻ ✻ ✻

It is now just more than two weeks since I attended
a most unusual evening worship service in Red Lodge,
Montana. It took place around a campfire on the banks of
Rock Creek on the property of Jim and Nancy Johnson, just
outside town.

Story referred to in Chapter 17

Worship is led by Jim, a former Lutheran pastor (ELCA)
turned bar owner. The people around the fire are bar people—the regulars from the Bull 'n Bear that Jim had run for
fifteen years and sold a little less than two years ago. Most of
them are not church people and have never attended church
regularly before. A few of them had been badly hurt in church
and have turned their back on it. The community around
the fire started from conversations in the bar and friendships
that evolved from spending time together in the Bull 'n Bear.
Most of them have only recently started reading the Bible.
The stories of the Bible are new to them. They do not know

how to 'behave' in church, the way people who were born into church do.

This is the birth of a church. Everything is fresh and new.

They arrive in ones and twos at Jim and Nancy's house. Before the start of the service we first have a beer or a glass of wine. The conversation is free and easy. Then we straggle out in the path to the clearing on the river bank.

The liturgy is run roughly along the basic lines of the Lutheran Church, but with many interjections by the people around the camp fire. This does not spoil the worship. It does quite the opposite. The comments are made naturally and unself-consciously. These are real people, without any of the religious veneer or the guardedness we have become so accustomed to in church.

Jim plays the guitar and we sing from folders he has prepared for the campfire services. Many of the songs have a country and western flavor to them. The people around the fire obviously enjoy them. A song with the rhythm and cord progression of "Hit the road, Jack" is sung, as is "All God's Critters" where there is spontaneous whooping during the chorus.

Jim reads Genesis 1 and gets to the sermon—a short exposition of the text that runs into an open conversation around the fire. Everyone participates. The text is not some-thing abstract or separate from ordinary daily experience. They draw from their own lives and the lives of others they all know in the discussion. Good things that have happened and small victories are all celebrated. Pain and brokenness is shared. And then we break the bread and share the wine. These are holy moments and we all know it.

What I experienced that evening in Red Lodge has filled me with hope for the church. It also asks some uncomfortable questions regarding the essence of church. Have we lost so much of the original genius of the church that the ordinary now seems exotic? Have we gotten so caught up in the externals that we have drifted away from the essentials? These are people doing church for the first time and they are getting it right. Then, why do we so often struggle with it?

We should not romanticize this little faith community, but we should realize the value of new creations of the Spirit like this and learn from them. Missional theology stresses the importance of spiritual discernment. We need to be on the lookout for what God is up to in this enchanted world we live in. But missional theology is not only about discernment; to a large extent it is discernment. It is also the study of these movements of the Spirit. We learn about God and his ways not only by studying the Bible and our faith tradition, but also from stories like those of Jim and his friends and their little community.

What do we learn when we are open to discern what God is doing in this community of faith? Here are some points of note that I would like to submit:

We learn about incarnational practices here.

Everything about this community is shaped by the specifics of the time and place and the persons that make up the fellowship. The story of the congregation is woven at the intersections of the real stories of these people's lives and the story of the God's commitment to this world we live in. We do not find commitment to some abstract ideal or theory of what church should be about. Something happened, something real. Flesh and blood people encountered God in the midst of the pain and joy that real life consists of. And the result was this community gathering on the banks of Rock Creek. Take away even one person, and it is a different community. Add even one more and it changes. This makes them alive to the fact that God is a part of everyday living. They know that He has brought them together and it is the most natural thing in the world for them to expect more encounters with Him when they disperse.

And here is an interesting point to ponder: For many of them the point of entry into the community was not salvation, but creation. Let me put it another way: they encountered God first of all in the mystery and wonder of daily existence and not through feeling the need to be saved. The things that first attracted them to God were "ordinary" things whose extraordinariness became clear to them: the birth of a calf, the beauty of the mountains, the caring touch of another human being—normal, everyday occurrences. God was never "out there" for them. Even if their pre-faith views about God were mostly fuzzy they knew that He was connected to the things they could touch and see.

This resonates with the creational theology of people like the Old Testament scholar Terence E. Fretheim. In his book *God and the World: a Relational Theology of Creation* he makes this very point. The Bible starts with the creation stories and persists with creation language. It never allows us to think of God as separate from or distant to our world. Our calling as living creatures is intimately connected to God's work of creation and blessing. We were placed here in this place and time for a reason. Frederick Buechner says somewhere that the two most important moments in your life are the day you were born and the day you discovered why.

Saying this does not make salvation redundant. It does, however, point to the fact that the way to salvation could start at many other points than the fear of damnation and a longing for heaven. Have we gotten so locked into our traditional views and evangelistic technology that we have boarded up the other doors that open into the kingdom of God? More about this under the next heading.

The incarnational nature of the Rock Creek community results in a peculiar brand of earthy spirituality. Connections between worship and life are never severed. There is (both literally and figuratively speaking) dirt on the hands that hold the Bible. Everyday life is taken seriously and spiritual talk is not about something other than our encounters with other people, work, eating and the good things that God blesses us with. Physical existence is never despised. The here and now is taken seriously, but with the expectancy that it will be transformed to be more than it is at present.

This is observable in the grounded and earthy language used, in the obvious enjoyment of physical blessings like food and wine (or beer), in the importance given to relationships. It is even the visible in the music. When a song resonates with a familiar showstopper, whooping during the chorus is not out of place in the least. Life is there to be enjoyed and this is not unspiritual in the least.

There is another side to this earthiness. Pain is not avoided, but faced. In actual fact, it is right there in the middle of the life of the community. It is reported, prayed for, faced, but with the knowledge that it is not ultimate. Religion is not escapism. It faces what needs to be faced. In fact, it presents us with the only way some things can be faced.

One could romanticize this community, but that would be missing the point completely. The most attractive feature displayed around the campfire that evening was their way of being, well, just people. Real people. There was a freedom to be themselves before God and in one another's company that was striking to an outsider like me.

Much of theology is anemic because of its tenuous attachment to the ordinariness of most of life in communities of faith. Getting to know communities like this can rescue us from our tendency towards abstraction. Walter Brueggemann, in his *Theology of the Old Testament*, proposes that we view the verbs Israel used when speaking of God as the core of their testimony. The adjectives and nouns are conclusions at a higher level of abstraction based on the things we can actually say that God did. If we lose the verbs, the attributes of God have a hollow and abstract ring to them. When we stay close to the work of the Spirit who gathers and shapes concrete faith communities, when we listen to their stories and learn from them, we reclaim the mighty verbs that express the nature of God. We lose our primary testimony to the world when we lose our stories.

This leads to my second observation:

We learn about discernment here.

Jim had told me many of the stories of the people I saw gathered while we were driving to Red Lodge for the worship service after some wonderful fly fishing on the Bighorn River. They were all stories of grace. God had entered their lives long before they even knew it and had been intimately involved with them. God gathered this community by attending personally to each of their lives.

The interesting thing about Jim's approach is this: the point of entry into the kingdom was not forced upon these people in Jim's conversations with them. Jim seemed almost to allow a form of "self-evangelism" by taking their cues and expanding on them. He plays the role of spiritual director by taking their questions and verbal prods over the bar counter and the poker table seriously. This reflects a basic belief regarding God's involvement in the world. Jim is convinced that God is at work in every human life and that this will be uncovered if we are only attentive enough. This is the basic belief and posture that lies behind all practices of spiritual discernment.

Ben Campbell Johnson wrote a book called *Speaking of God* a number of years ago where he champions exactly this approach to evangelism. The sub-title of the book is evangelism as initial spiritual direction. He proposes that we rethink evangelism along the lines of spiritual direction; that we assume that God is already at work in the life of every person we encounter. We should learn to listen expectantly to pick up on what God is up to in the lives of others. Our task as evangelists is to help people recognize this as the work of God.

This is what Jim has been doing all along. Maybe no other approach would have been respectful enough of God's work to help these people recognize it in themselves. A traditional confrontational approach would, in all probability, simply have scared most of these people away or led to stubborn resistance.

The processes of discernment practiced here are not limited to evangelism and occurrences in the lives of individuals. God not only nudged individuals towards faith, but He also brought them together into a community. Their story teaches us much about discernment at collective level. The almost tentative nature in which they started coming together—at first only twice a year and then bi-weekly—is also a story of being gently guided into something by the Spirit. God leads us towards his will, but does not violate us in the process. He is ever patient with us. When Jim and Nancy started feeling the need to gather friends together for worship during Christmas and Easter time was ripe for people to join them. Bonds of trust had been establish that were strong enough to overcome the obstacles that would have prevented this from succeeding earlier on. It is only fitting that the idea to start meeting every second week was born from Terri's desire to be baptized. Baptism, after all, incorporates one into the body of Christ. In a sense the whole group was inserted into the body on that day. The Spirit had been prodding and leading them for some time before that day and what came about received its shape and vitality from Him.

This community, then, did not come into existence by technical means. It is not the result of some heroic individual getting vital information from the books and applying it in skilled ways. The story told by Jim and the others is one of being pulled into a joint relationship with the Triune God by God Himself.

So, Jim did not strategize. This says nothing against strategy and taking the initiative. It does, however, uncover the basic posture one should have, with or without strategies. The posture is one of receptivity—receptivity towards God and His initiative, but also receptivity towards others, however unlikely, as people in whom God is at work. This, in a nutshell, is what all the talk about discernment boils down to. Having this posture does not give us license to be lax in regard to what we put into the community. Being a community requires hard work. It requires that we tend to our relationships with God and others, inside and outside the community. This often requires strenuous effort. What this posture does, though, is to keep us aware of the true source of the coming of the kingdom of God. It is always an inbreaking of the Spirit. It is never our accomplishment, no matter how much hard work we have put in.

This posture gives the community two characteristics. Firstly, it seems very fragile. It has no buildings or paid staff to give the impression of permanence. It has no sure-fire recipe for being church that they project with cocksure confidence. Instead, there is a steady reliance and belief that the intangibles of church are the most reliable. It matches the description of faith in Hebrews 11:1 as "being sure of what we hope for and certain of what we do not see." This makes it enduring in spite of its fragility. If there is any confidence in the community, it is firmly placed on God, the rock. This is the result of discernment taking such a central place.

In addition, it is not spectacular. It is not a huge crowd of people in a glitzy building with all the best gadgets and an impressive array of programs. It did not come into being in dramatic and eye-catching ways, but in the small and personal ways in which the Spirit mostly works his way. The community was formed through many little conversations and acts of caring on the part of Jim and Nancy and also among the people themselves. It is not an ego-booster for leadership and members, but it is thoroughly human. It revels in the ordinary. This makes it approachable and real. This also translates effortlessly to an understanding of one's own very ordinary life as a place where the Spirit is present and actively involved. Church and life are not separated into two zones—the secular and the holy. In both church and in our lives the ordinary and the holy are enmeshed. We are always on holy ground.

This reveals the community to us not as a project to be imitated, but as companions on a journey of discernment. What we learn from them is to pay attention to what God is doing in our own lives and community and to continue trusting that He will guide us in ways that fit our circumstances.

The important thing is the posture of receptivity to the work of the Spirit.

This community is on an adventure of discovery. They have no long-term goals and plans. They are open to surprises. Of course the Spirit often leads through goals and plans. That will probably come later in their life as a faith community. It is also true that turning the church into a project leads us to be less open to the Spirit's proddings in many cases. The visions promoted by leaders in institutional church settings are always in danger of becoming personal ambitions. Therefore processes of discernment need to be central for any faith community. We need habits and practices that keep us attentive to the Spirit's guidance and that safeguard us against our propensity to take charge ourselves.

We learn about the relational nature of the work of the Spirit here.

My third observation is about the nature of the community I encountered at Rock Creek. I have already alluded to it in my previous observation: the relational nature of the work of the Spirit is in evidence here. One's first and overpowering impression of the community is of the easy and natural way of their relationships to each other. This is not a community of whole people and they would, in all likelihood, protest any attempt at describing them as such. Some of the people have gone through life-shattering experiences and many of them face ongoing struggles. This is, though, a healthy community. People are valued as persons and not for the contributions they can make or for the outstanding attributes they display. They are given the freedom to be themselves and accepted as such. This kind of community is a rare thing in our time.

This is not something contrived. The community grew conversation by conversation, relationship by relationship, bit by bit. All of the relationships preceded the first gatherings on the banks of Rock Creek by many years. God starts his work long before we are even inadvertently involved. And even when we get involved, it usually takes some time before we catch on to what is going on. Sometimes, I think, the work is finished long before we even realize that we have participated in the movement of the Spirit.

Missional theology tells us that this is a sign that it is the Triune God at work. God is a relational being. The three Persons are in community with one another and they are endlessly inviting their creatures into this community. Therefore we will not find God at work in the world as an impersonal power, using brute strength to impose Himself on us.

We learn about being a missional church here.

The relational nature of the community gives it a strong missional openness. These are people who have answered God's invitation into his communal life and, by being shaped by this, have become invitational themselves. They are not a clique. They have an understanding of church that is inclusive from the start. Two of us around the fire that evening were strangers to them. This did not inhibit them in any way. In fact, we were invited into the conversation. They wanted to hear our thoughts and they kept the conversation going long after the worship service had ended. This is a most attractive feature for a church and construes it as a hospitable church open to strangers.

Many other features of the community also add to its missional nature. The shape of the liturgy is in close proximity to the culture of their context, though distinctly Christian. This goes for the socializing before and after worship, the music, the setting, the dress code and the language used. The language is not churchy or formal. A person with no background of churchgoing will have no trouble following the liturgy or participating in the conversations.

Congregations consisting of people that had grown up in church tend to form a culture that runs parallel with existing culture. We develop language, rituals and ways of doing things that are intimidating to first-timers. I was alerted to this fact again by experiencing its opposite at Rock Creek.

We learn about kenotic leadership here.

Jesus' approach to leadership was not based on power. Quite the opposite. In Matthew 20:25-28 Jesus tells his disciples, "You know that the rulers of the Gentiles lord it over them, and their high officials exercise authority over them. Not so with you. Instead, whoever wants to become great among you must be your servant, and whoever wants to be first must be your slave—just as the Son of Man did not come to be served, but to serve, and to give his life as a ransom for many." Jesus' self-giving sacrifice sets the tone for leadership in the church. Perhaps the strongest pronouncement along these lines are found in Philippians 2 where Paul holds up Jesus' laying down (kenosis) of his heavenly status as something to be emulated by all Christians.

Jim's role in the community was pivotal from the start. When we compare his story and the role he plays in the community with those of the leaders of prominent church plants elsewhere, though, the differences are striking. Jim did not arrive on the scene as a person with grand ideas and a billboard reputation. He came as a former priest with a failed marriage and the new owner of a bar. Jim probably thought of himself as a failure as far as the work of ministry is concerned. But from this "failure" God wrought something new.

Jim's own story is a story of descent. His loss of his status as pastor, his shame and leaving church stripped him of almost all of the conventional means of reaching out to people with the gospel and of starting a church. This could have led to him and Nancy (who shared this descent with him) to finally turn their backs on God and religious society. Of course, we should have known that God often works his way through our defeats and brokenness. In the end it turned out to be a key element that allowed the story of this congregation to unfold. This allowed Jim and Nancy to get close enough to these people to do Christian ministry. On the one hand Jim's story made him 'safe' and approachable to people who expect to be shamed by pastors. On the other hand he was still, for them, the religious expert—the one who knew God. This unusual combination led to many conversations and remarks that planted the seeds for the community. The very anomaly of a former priest as a bar owner was a key to his new ministry.

Missional leadership needs to be essentially kenotic. John of the Cross taught us lucidly that God often uses a dark night of the soul to shape us for ministry. Our ways of relating to power need to emulate Jesus' self-emptying. The ethic of missional leadership is one of self-sacrifice and the story of Jim's ministry is a vivid demonstration of an authentic way in which this can be done. Few of us will be asked to walk the painful path of rejection in the way Jim had to do it, but we should be forewarned that leadership in missional churches cannot be anything other than cross-bearing. Stories of leaders may differ, but following Jesus will always be following the crucified Lord.

There is much more that can be learned by observing this extraordinary community of ordinary people. Of course, no-one can do that better than Jim himself. Jim and this community are a gift to the Christian church at large—not as something to be copied, but as a listening-post where the whispering voice of the Spirit can be heard. I am grateful that we now have this collection of stories and theological musing in written form. May this work in progress stay true to its nature as the work of God the Spirit.

*To Learn more about the Missional Church or
to read more about the subject, contact us at:*

CHURCH
INNOVATIONS

1563 Como Avenue, #103
St Paul, Mn 55108
651-644-3653 or 888-223-7631

or visit:

www.churchinnovations.org

ORIGINAL MUSIC CD'S BY JIM JOHNSON

JIM · JOHNSON

Rachel's Lament (5:01)
Megan's Song (3:23)
Falling (Ps. 13) (4:20)
The Water Is Wide (2:33)
What Every Drifter Knows (5:02)
Still My Love (3:43)
A Hard Case (5:52)
A Rose For Me (3:48)
In The Presence of a Miracle (3:54)
A Child Like Me (3:47)
The Lord's Prayer (2:25)

©1995 Eighth Day Creations Music,
Box 575, Red Lodge, Montana 59068.
All rights reserved.
Unauthorized duplication is a violation
of applicable laws.

Real · Life

The Fathers' Heart

Jim Johnson

"Jim Johnson's music is a breath of fresh air. Songs like 'Rachel's Lament' can treat serious subjects without being heavy or sentimental; others like 'Megan's Song' capture the uncomplicated joy of a child. Best of all, perhaps, is that one can listen to a whole album of religious music without feeling burdened: while not denying the darkness, Johnson writes and sings about life lived in the light of God's promises."

—DONALD JUEL, **Professor of NT**

Princeton Theological Seminary

"Much of today's Christian music seems to rush past the cross in order to arrive at the joy of the resurrection. Not so Jim Johnson. His beautiful songs face squarely the pain and grief of our hurting world—those occasions where faith and life intersect, indeed, sometimes collide—as they comfort and inspire us with the assurance of God's unfailing love and grace."

—STAN LYNDE, **artist and author**

"The music is fresh. The lyrics resonate with the sounds of life and a deep sensitivity to the Christian theology of the Cross."

—MARK RAMSETH, **former bishop**

Montana Synod ELCA

THE FATHERS' HEART:
The Fathers' Heart
The River of Life
Morning
What He Wants of Me
From: Mathew 6
Come Feast your Eyes
Open your Eyes
Servant Song
In the End
Rain a Little While

REAL LIFE
Rachel's Lament
A Hard Case
Megan's Song
A Rose For Me
Falling
In the Presence of a Miracle
The Water is Wide
A Child Like Me
What Every Drifter Knows
The Lord's Prayer
Still My Love

CDs + Cassettes available at:
www.churchinnovations.org
(click the Music tab in the store)

JIM JOHNSON was born in north western Montana. He holds a Bachelor of Music in Theory and Composition degree from Pacific Lutheran University, and after receiving an M. Div. degree from Luther Seminary served as an ELCA Lutheran pastor for 10 years. With his wife Nancy, he (once again) owns and operates the Bull'n Bear Saloon in Red Lodge, Montana, where he and Nancy currently reside.

Jim is available for concert/speaking engagements, and can be reached directly at **8thday10@gmail.com**